604

✦✦✦✦✦✦✦✦✦✦✦✦✦✦✦✦✦✦

BASEBALL
SUPERSTARS

Mickey Mantle

✦✦✦✦✦✦✦✦✦✦✦✦✦✦✦✦✦✦

Hank Aaron
Ty Cobb
Johnny Damon
Lou Gehrig
Rickey Henderson
Derek Jeter
Randy Johnson
Andruw Jones
Mickey Mantle
Roger Maris

Mike Piazza
Kirby Puckett
Albert Pujols
Mariano Rivera
Jackie Robinson
Babe Ruth
Curt Schilling
Ichiro Suzuki
Bernie Williams
Ted Williams

✳✷✳✷✳✷✳✷✳✷✳✷✳✷✳✷✳✷✳✷✳✷✳

BASEBALL SUPERSTARS

Mickey Mantle

Ronald A. Reis

CHELSEA HOUSE
PUBLISHERS
An imprint of Infobase Publishing

✳✷✳✷✳✷✳✷✳✷✳✷✳✷✳✷✳✷✳✷✳✷✳

MICKEY MANTLE

Copyright © 2008 by Infobase Publishing

All rights reserved. No part of this book may be reproduced or utilized in any form or by any means, electronic or mechanical, including photocopying, recording, or by any information storage or retrieval systems, without permission in writing from the publisher. For information, contact:

Chelsea House
An imprint of Infobase Publishing
132 West 31st Street
New York NY 10001

Library of Congress Cataloging-in-Publication Data
Reis, Ronald A., 1941–
  Mickey Mantle / Ronald A. Reis.
     p. cm. — (Baseball superstars)
  Includes bibliographical references and index.
  ISBN 978-0-7910-9546-1 (hardcover)
  1. Mantle, Mickey, 1931–1995. 2. Baseball players—United States—Biography.
3. New York Yankees (Baseball team) I. Title. II. Series.
  GV865.M36R45 2008
  796.357092—dc22
  [B]   2007028937

Chelsea House books are available at special discounts when purchased in bulk quantities for businesses, associations, institutions, or sales promotions. Please call our Special Sales Department in New York at (212) 967-8800 or (800) 322-8755.

You can find Chelsea House on the World Wide Web at http://www.chelseahouse.com

Series design by Erik Lindstrom
Cover design by Ben Peterson

Printed in the United States of America

Bang EJB 10 9 8 7 6 5 4 3 2 1

This book is printed on acid-free paper.

All links and Web addresses were checked and verified to be correct at the time of publication. Because of the dynamic nature of the Web, some addresses and links may have changed since publication and may no longer be valid.

CONTENTS

Father Knows Best

It was a brisk October day, one that saw Commerce High School sophomore Mickey Mantle charging hard, playing his second-favorite sport—football. Cradling the ball low, the darting 14-year-old halfback never saw him coming, the tackler who accidentally kicked Mickey on the left shin. What followed soon after almost ended Mickey Mantle's future professional career—as a baseball player.

Helping the obviously pained Mickey off the field, the coach assured his star competitor that it was only a sprain. By the next morning, though, the boy's temperature had soared to 104 degrees. His ankle had ballooned to twice its normal size. Taken to American Hospital in nearby Picher, Oklahoma, the local doctor, D. L. Connell, lanced Mickey's ankle. Days later, the infection remained. In a desperate measure, squirming maggots were "sprinkled" directly on the inflamed area in the hope they would devour the invading toxic bacteria. With no improvement, Connell gathered Mickey's parents. "The bone is badly abscessed," he told them, as reported in *The Mick*, Mantle's 1985 autobiography. "I'm afraid it is osteomyelitis. We may have to amputate the leg."

"You ain't taking his leg off," Lovell, Mickey's mother, cried, as quoted in *Mickey Mantle: Before the Glory*.

"There isn't any place in the world for a one-legged man," Mickey's father, Mutt, echoed. Rushing their desperately ill son out of Picher, the Mantles headed straight to Children's Hospital, 175 miles (282 kilometers) away in Oklahoma City.

For 19 days, every three hours, around the clock, a frightened and alone Mickey Mantle was injected with a new wonder drug, penicillin, released for wide distribution only a year before, in 1945. Boils, 15 to 20, covered his body. The sickly, runt-looking Mantle fell to 110 pounds (50 kilograms) from a weight of a little more than 130 pounds (59 kilograms).

Then, after an agonizing few weeks, the turnaround began. Mickey's appetite improved. His weight increased dramatically. And the boils that were all over his legs, arms, and even his eyes, disappeared.

Osteomyelitis, however, would remain with Mickey Mantle all his life. The inflammatory bone disease could be temporarily arrested but never completely cured. The affliction would be but one of many debilitating conditions that dogged the future Yankee All-Star throughout his 18 years in the majors.

Upon release from the hospital, Mickey headed home to rural Ottawa County, Oklahoma, crutches under his arms. There would be a few basketball games to play between flare-ups and even a return to football. The course, though, was clear. From now on, the one true sport in Mickey Mantle's future would be the one he loved most of all—baseball.

A FATHER'S OBSESSION

According to Mickey's mother, within 12 hours of his birth, on October 20, 1931, in Spavinaw, Oklahoma, a baseball was placed in his hands while he lay in his crib. In the days to come, the ball was followed by a mitt, all the better for the baby to chew on. Dad, it is said, insisted that his first son, named after Mickey Cochrane, a major-league player with the Philadelphia Athletics, be taught the positions on the baseball field before the ABCs. Mickey Mantle was born to be a baseball player.

Mom and Dad formed an odd couple. Lovell Thomas, Mickey's mother, ran off, at the age of 17, to marry William Theodore Davis. She would have two children by this first marriage before the inevitable divorce.

Mickey's father, Elvin Clark Mantle (known as Mutt from birth), was 10 years younger than Lovell when he began to court her. Having quit school to help out his financially strapped family, Mutt was only 17 and grading country roads when he asked the grown woman, Lovell, to marry him. "He had been tall, handsome, and a real gentleman under the rough exterior," Mickey's mother was to have reported decades later, as recorded in *Mickey Mantle: America's Prodigal Son*, written by Tony Castro. Strange as the union seemed, the marriage worked.

Despite some differences, Mickey's parents shared a love of baseball. Mutt, no matter how tired he was from working on the roads and in the zinc mines of northeastern Oklahoma, found time to play semipro baseball on the weekends. That was as far as it would go, however; no professional scouts ever saw Mutt swing a bat. Had they, he, rather than his son, might have been the Mantle to make it to the majors.

Mom, an avid fan with an eye (actually an ear) for detail, followed the game closely on the radio. "While my mother washed and ironed clothes, she always had a yellow writing

Elvin "Mutt" Mantle sits with his toddler son, Mickey, on the porch of their home in Oklahoma. Mutt Mantle was an avid baseball fan and reportedly made sure that Mickey knew the positions on the baseball field before his ABCs. Mickey was named after Mickey Cochrane, a star player with the Philadelphia Athletics whom Mutt admired.

tablet near the ironing board," Mickey recalled in his book *All My Octobers*. "When my dad came home from the mines, close to nightfall, she could tell him everything he missed."

Poor but hardworking, the Mantles, in the Great Depression of the 1930s, still found time to take in America's pastime—baseball. For Mickey, however, it would involve far more than listening to games on the radio or an occasional road trip to St. Louis to see a Cardinals contest. It would include play, play, play, all the better to prepare for the day when baseball would become his life's work.

"SCREEN APE"

The Great Depression, which saw as many as one in four adult Americans out of work, was a national economic disaster. For those living in the Midwest, particularly in states like Oklahoma, there was the added devastation of the Dust Bowl. Caused by the misuse of the land and years of drought, the Southern Plains region saw soil literally stripped away, with farming all but impossible. Nothing would grow. Those who could, left, to be forever referred to as "Okies."

"As a five- or six-year-old, I would stand in the front yard watching the cars and trucks go by with people jammed in and water jugs banging against the sides," Mantle recalled in *All My Octobers*. "They were all heading the same way—west. In the summer, nights following the days, we slept with a wet washrag over our faces to filter out the dust."

Mickey's family, however, did not join in the Okie migration. Mutt insisted that they stay put, the better to eke out a living in the region's lead and zinc mines. Doing so was hard and dangerous work. If a cave-in did not end your days, "miner's disease" often would. Being underground eight hours a day, breathing in the dust and dampness, and coughing up gobs of phlegm were bound to take their toll.

Later, in the summers of his teenage years, Mickey would often work with his father's crew, dropping 400 feet (122 meters) into the earth, deep into Oklahoma. At other times, he would work as a "screen ape," smashing large rocks into small stones with a sledgehammer. Clearly, all that pounding was responsible for the incredibly strong wrists,

☆ ☆ ☆ ☆ ☆
BLOWN IN THE WIND: AMERICA'S DUST BOWL OF THE 1930s

The cyclic winds rolled up two miles (3.2 kilometers) high and spread 100 miles (161 kilometers) wide. They roared ahead at more than 60 miles per hour (97 kilometers per hour), engulfing fleeing birds in their way. Many believed the world was coming to an end.

On April 14, 1935, which is known as Black Sunday, the worst Dust Bowl cloud had turned day into night. The storm destroyed vast areas of Great Plains farmland, from Denver to Oklahoma City and beyond. Witnesses reported that they could not see five feet in front of them.

A year earlier, on May 11, 1934, a similar storm blew all the way to Chicago, dumping 12 million pounds of powdered soil, the equivalent of four pounds of dirt per person, on the Windy City. Remnants of the same storm actually reached the East Coast—New York and Washington, D.C.—and even a ship at sea, 300 miles (483 kilometers) off the Atlantic Coast. That year, red snow fell in New England.

In an attempt to survive the onrushing dust-filled winds, men, women, and children sealed themselves indoors, tying water-soaked handkerchiefs around their noses and mouths and hanging damp sheets over their beds. If people dared to leave their houses, they wore goggles to protect their eyes.

shoulders, arms, and forearms for which Mickey would become famous.

Yet the way forward, out of the mines, with their threat of disease and injury, would not be via hefting a sledgehammer. For Mickey Mantle, it would be through swinging a bat.

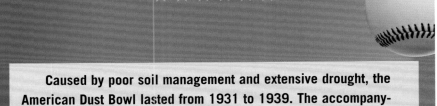

Caused by poor soil management and extensive drought, the American Dust Bowl lasted from 1931 to 1939. The accompanying dry spell was the worst in U.S. history, covering more than 75 percent of the country and affecting 27 states. In one year alone, 1934, more than 100 million acres in crops were lost because of soil erosion. In the following year, it is estimated that 850 million tons of topsoil were blown off the Southern Plains of the United States. In some parts of the country, "dirt days," as they had come to be called, occurred more than 50 percent of the year.

Oklahoma, where Mickey Mantle was living at the time, suffered severely. About 15 percent of the state's 2.3 million residents, 300,000 to 400,000, packed up and left. Known as Okies, they headed west, desperately looking for work and new land. They were not always welcomed as they trekked onward, dragging all they owned with them. In February 1936, Los Angeles Police Chief James E. Davis sent 125 policemen to patrol the state's borders, all the better to keep the oncoming "undesirables" out. Mercifully, the rains came in 1939, ending the "Dirty Thirties" nightmare.

Today, with modern soil-conservation methods in place, there is little likelihood of a renewed Dust Bowl era. Though when it comes to nature, one can never be sure.

BAXTER SPRINGS WHIZ KIDS

If Mutt Mantle could not become a professional baseball player, he was determined that his eldest son would. To that end, both parents encouraged young Mickey to take off whenever time permitted to just play the game. "There were days when I left home with nothing more than a Thermos jug of water, to play ball from breakfast until dark, without even a break for food, and my parents sent me off with their blessing," Mantle recalled in his 1967 autobiography, *Mickey Mantle: The Education of a Baseball Player*. For days on end, Mickey would play the "Alkali" fields near his home, where bases were often made of cow dung and the outfield went on and on, unbroken to the backyards of Commerce.

Mickey believed that in his early years there was no special skill that made him the baseball standout he was. Rather, it was his love of the game, plus his desire and need to please his father, that gave him his success.

A key factor in Mickey's baseball accomplishments, as a kid and later as a professional, was the ability to switch-hit—bat left or right. For hours, Mutt, a left-hander, would pitch to Mickey, a natural right-hander. Then Grandpa Charlie, a right-hander, would take over and pitch to Mickey, as he stood at the plate as a left-handed hitter. "For a long time it was awkward and difficult for me to bat left-handed, but my father would not let me quit," Mantle remembered in *Mickey Mantle: The Education of a Baseball Player*. Mutt calculated that switch-hitters were a valuable commodity in professional baseball and would get more turns at bat. Father was right. Father knew best.

By the time Mickey turned 11, he was playing in organized baseball in the local Gabby Street League. Hundreds would show up on a lazy afternoon to see the youngsters play in what was then the equivalent of today's Little League.

On into high school, Mickey played many sports, notably football. Though Mickey played some baseball for Commerce High, it was as a Baxter Springs Whiz Kid, in the Ban Johnson

Mickey Mantle is seen in a picture from around 1945 when he played for a team in Miami, Oklahoma. As a teenager, his speed and his ability as a power hitter began to attract the attention of professional scouts.

League, that the now 16-year-old came into his own as a power player.

The Whiz Kids were a highly competitive semipro team consisting of the best players frowm Kansas, Oklahoma, and Missouri. Having recovered from his bout with osteomyelitis, Mickey had grown strong, with an upper-body strength that saw him smacking balls way into the outfield, some 400 feet (122 meters) or more. And he was fast, mighty fast. Some say Mickey developed such speed by running home at dark, along spooky dirt roads, afraid of what might jump out at him. Later, as a rookie with the New York Yankees, Mickey would be timed in an incredible 3.00 seconds sprinting from home plate to first base.

Though a bit of a fumbler in the field (whether playing second base or shortstop), as high school graduation approached, Mickey Mantle, now dubbed "The Commerce Comet," had become a forceful hitter with speed to match. Professional scouts had taken notice.

A CONTRACT IS SIGNED

On Friday, May 27, 1949, Mickey Mantle received his high school diploma. He did not, however, attend the evening's graduation ceremonies. Having obtained permission from Bentley Baker, the Commerce High School principal, Mickey was off playing baseball with the Baxter Springs Whiz Kids against the Coffeyville Refiners, in nearby Coffeyville, Kansas. Knowing that Tom Greenwade, a local Yankee scout, would be in the stands, Mickey did not want to miss the chance to impress. Batting right-handed against a left-handed pitcher, he went four for five with two singles, a double, and a home run. Baxter Springs won the game, 13-7.

Greenwade had been waiting until Mickey actually graduated before officially "looking" at him. According to the rules of organized baseball at the time, a scout was forbidden to approach an athlete still in high school. By all accounts,

Greenwade liked what he saw of Mickey that Friday night. But when he buttonholed Mutt and his son after the game, Greenwade played it coy. "I'm afraid Mickey may never reach the Yankees," he said, as quoted in *The Mick.* "Right now, I'd have to rate him a lousy shortstop. Sloppy. Erratic arm. And he's small. Get him in front of some really strong pitching. . . ."

Was Greenwade telling the truth, though? Later, after a contract was signed, he told the press that Mantle would probably set records with the Yankees, equaling Babe Ruth's and Joe DiMaggio's marks. Greenwade, it would seem, was out to lowball Mickey and his dad.

On Sunday, May 29, 1949, after another game that Greenwade observed, Mickey, Mutt, and Greenwade huddled in the scout's car, rain pounding the roof. In 15 minutes, a provisional contract was signed. The Yankees organization picked up Mickey Mantle, *the* Mickey Mantle, for all of $1,500. It was a simple breakdown: $400 for playing out the rest of the summer in Class D ball with the Independence Yankees of Independence, Kansas, in the K-O-M League, and a $1,100 signing bonus.

Mickey felt that he and his father had been "outslicked," as Mickey said in his 1967 autobiography. Greenwade, as far as father and son saw it, had engineered one of the greatest signing coups in sports history.

The Yankee scout, however, had a different perspective. Years later, Greenwade said (as published in *Our Mickey: Cherished Memories of an American Icon*), "I always told the press he was the greatest I ever saw. It really wasn't so. I was always concerned about whether or not the Yankees could find a position for him. It was a good thing they moved him to the outfield."

That aside, Mickey Mantle was now ready to play professional baseball. And although it would be for a Class D team (the lowest rung on the minor-league ladder), it was for the Yankees organization. From the Independence Yankees to the "real" Yankees, how far could that be?

Country Bumpkin

On June 13, 1949, Mickey Mantle arrived in Independence, Kansas, to play Class D ball for the Independence Yankees, the "Baby Yanks," of the K-O-M (Kansas-Oklahoma-Missouri) League. "I've done all I can for Mickey," Mutt told Harry Craft, the team manager, as reported in *The Mick*. "I believe he's a good ballplayer, and I'm turning him over to you now." As Mutt moved to leave, he added, "This is your chance, son. Take care of yourself and give 'em hell."

The next day, Mickey played his first professional baseball game. "Up to then, I'd outdistanced the other kids by a mile," Mantle recalled in his second autobiography, *The Mick*. "But now I was a pro, and the competition got a lot stiffer. . . . I had to learn that I was going to make seven outs for every 10 times at bat."

Though universally recognized to be a poor, if not down-right lousy, shortstop, Mantle finished his first pro season with a .313 batting average in 89 games. He led the league in hitting.

The next year, Mantle was moved up a notch to play Class C ball with the Joplin Miners of the Western Association. Before regular-season play, the "Commerce Comet" got a lucky break. Mantle was sent to spring training in St. Petersburg, Florida, to hit and catch with the major-league Yankees.

Virtually unknown to the New York management, Mantle, nonetheless, was impressive at the plate. Hitting from both sides, his shots were going out farther than anyone could remember seeing balls fly in spring training. After a particularly mighty blast, manager Casey Stengel was said to have yelled, as reported in *Mickey Mantle: America's Prodigal Son*, "What'sis name? Mantle?"

Back in Joplin, Missouri, for the regular season, Mantle had an unbelievable year. Playing in 137 games, he batted .383, with 26 home runs and 136 RBIs. Then, when the minor-league season ended, the 18-year-old was called up to join the New York Yankees for a series against the Browns in St. Louis, on their final two-week road trip.

Though he was a non-roster player and saw no action in any game, Mantle was now in earshot and full view of his pro idol, Joe DiMaggio. They did not speak. "With Joe DiMaggio I couldn't even mumble hello," Mantle recalled in *The Mick*. "He had this aura. It was as if you needed an appointment just to approach him."

It was late in the year, yet Mantle was getting a taste of the majors. And the big leaguers were getting an eyeful of him.

MAKING AN IMPRESSION

Mantle had become a prospect, and a hot one at that. Yet what to do with him? To bring a Class C player up to the majors, even if just for instructional camp, was a stretch. As James Dawson of the *New York Times* pointed out on February 24, 1951, "Despite his spectacular record with Joplin, Mantle faces the tradition that few rookies ever have gone from Class C to the majors in one leap."

Yet Stengel had seen enough of Mantle in the spring and fall of 1950 to want him in 1951 at the Yankees' new training

★ ★ ★ ★ ☆

MINOR STUFF

The year Mickey Mantle began his professional baseball career, the minor leagues reached the apex of their golden age. In 1949, there were 59 leagues and 448 clubs, an all-time high. The same year, attendance reached 39,640,433, a figure that would stand for the next 54 years. During the post-World War II period, from 1946 to 1952, before the advent of television and major-league expansion, folks in small-town America and those west of the Mississippi River could not get enough of baseball, major or minor league.

The K-O-M League, in which Mantle played in 1949, was just one of 24 Class D leagues in operation that year. With each league fielding six to eight teams, close to 200 Class D ball clubs were active across the country. Some leagues had colorful names, such as Blue Ridge, Kitty, Longhorn, Pony, and Tobacco State. With the exception of one Class E league, the Twin Ports League, formed in 1943, all Class D players looked up from the bottom, at leagues with a higher ranking. Class D ball was professional baseball, but just barely.

In 1901, the National Association of Professional Baseball Leagues was formed, and thus the birth of the minor leagues. In

camp in Phoenix, Arizona. Mantle was sent a letter telling him to show up.

In mid-February, however, the 5-foot-10-inch, 175-pound Mantle was nowhere to be found. Stengel was irate. Truth be known, Mantle could not afford to make the trip. "They didn't send no ticket or nothing," Mantle was to relate later in *The Mick*. He was expecting that the Yankees would send him a

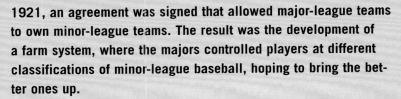

1921, an agreement was signed that allowed major-league teams to own minor-league teams. The result was the development of a farm system, where the majors controlled players at different classifications of minor-league baseball, hoping to bring the better ones up.

The largest crowd to appear at a minor-league game arrived at Mile High Stadium in Denver on July 4, 1982. A grand total of 65,666 fans watched an American Association game followed by a giant fireworks show.

In 1991, minimum standards for minor-league ballparks were established. As a result, new stadiums sprang up everywhere. Today, more than half the teams in the minors play in stadiums built or completely renovated since 1991.

Here is the current minor-league classification system:

AAA (highest classification; also called Triple A)

AA (second-highest classification; also called Double A)

A–Advanced (third-highest classification; also called High A)

A (fourth-highest classification; also called Low A)

A–Short Season (fifth-highest classification)

Rookie (lowest classification)

In 1950, Mickey Mantle's second season in the Yankees' farm system, he played for the Joplin Miners of the Class C Western Association. He batted .383 for the year and joined the Yankees at the end of the season for a two-week road trip. Mantle did not play, but he soaked in the major-league atmosphere.

ticket for transportation and a check for expenses. A few days later, scout Tom Greenwade arrived in Commerce with both.

Within hours, Mantle was on his way west, beat-up suitcase in hand. "I climbed aboard the train, pausing to wave, panic-stricken at the thought that winning a trip to the Yankees' first school for farm prospects would end in disaster," he recalled in *The Mick*. "An awful realization, despite the raves over my hitting performance at Joplin the previous season."

In camp, Mantle hit the ground running—literally. The 19-year-old's speed had already been glimpsed the previous year, in the spring and fall. Now, though, Mantle was outrunning everyone. Taking off from the right-handed hitter's side of the plate, he was clocked at 3.1 seconds to first base. From the other side of the plate, he made it even faster, in 3.0 seconds. It is fair to say that at this point, Mickey Mantle was the fastest player in baseball—period.

Running like a demon, displaying his awesome switch-hitting talent, Mantle was impressive—at the plate. At short-stop, however, there was less to get excited about. Teammate Phil Rizzuto would claim that Mantle threw most of the balls from shortstop into the stands.

The solution was obvious. Stengel approached his now-favorite rookie. "Ever think of playing the outfield?" he asked, as reported in *Mickey Mantle: The Education of a Baseball Player*. Mantle, always willing to be a team player, reasoned that, as he was to say later, "If you can move fast and throw better than your grandmother, you can be an outfielder."

As the 1951 exhibition season got under way, Stengel put Mantle in center field. He would play his first game as a Yankee in the position still reserved for Joe DiMaggio.

EXHIBITION BALL

Babe Ruth, Lou Gehrig, and Joe DiMaggio all rolled into one—that was how Stengel and the newspaper reporters who crowded spring-training camp were hailing the young, bemused Mickey Mantle. "I wasn't what Casey said I was," Mantle reflected some time later, in Castro's biography. "I don't mind admitting that there was incredible pressure on me because of what Casey was saying, and the fans were expecting so much, which I wasn't able to deliver."

With instruction camp ending, the Yankees took Mantle with them on an 11-game exhibition swing through California, where they played Pacific Coast League clubs and university teams. Mantle tore the leather off the ball.

In one momentous game against the University of Southern California (USC) on March 26, Mantle smashed two home runs, a triple, and a single. One of those homers took off as if into orbit. It left the ballpark at the 439-foot sign, cleared the football field behind it, and crash-landed an estimated 650 feet (198 meters) from where it was launched. There were those on the field that day who would later claim it was the farthest they had ever seen a baseball hit.

Returning from the West Coast, Mantle was upbeat, but he expected to be sent off to the minors for another year. "I had no fault to find with my fate just then," he recalled in *Mickey Mantle: The Education of a Baseball Player*. "I had stayed with the big club longer than I had expected. I was all over my homesickness, and I felt strong and hopeful, ready for anything Casey Stengel might send my way."

What Stengel sent his way nearly blew him away. "How would you like to stay with the Yankees?" the 60-year-old manager asked Mantle, as recorded in Mantle's 1967 autobiography. The team, now on the East Coast, was speeding by train from New York City to Washington D.C., on April 15, for the season opener. General manager George Weiss, however, was against Mantle playing in the majors so soon. He wanted the youngster on a Class AAA team, maybe in Kansas City, at least for another year.

Stengel, though, was adamant in feeling that 19-year-old Mickey Mantle was ready for the majors. "I don't care if he's in diapers," Stengel told Weiss, as reported in Castro's biography. Mantle stood dumbstruck at his manager's side, cigar smoke rising in the private lounge. "If he's good enough to play for us on a regular basis, I want to keep him."

Mickey Mantle attended the Yankees' spring-training camp in 1951 in Phoenix, Arizona, and joined the team for an exhibition swing along the West Coast. Here, he warmed up on March 21 in Los Angeles. During a game five days later against the University of Southern California, he hit two home runs, including one that traveled roughly 650 feet.

Weiss, with the blessings of Yankees owners Del Webb and Dan Topping, relented. Then and there, Mickey Mantle signed a rookie contract for $7,500, just $2,500 above the minimum. The ecstatic Mantle had become a "real" Yankee.

UNFIT TO SERVE

Mantle was now ready to go; ready to play big-league ball. There was a problem, however. Uncle Sam wanted Mantle to go, too—go to war.

On June 25, 1950, 135,000 North Korean troops stormed across the 38th parallel, invading South Korea. Though referred to throughout the three-year conflict as a "police action," the United States was now at war. The country needed able-bodied fighting men, and plenty of them. Athletes were expected to "step up to the plate," given their visibility and excellent physical shape. Surely a 19-year-old boy, who was demonstrating every day what he could do with a ball and a bat, would be a prime candidate for military service? Evidently not.

In December 1950, Mantle was ordered by his Ottawa County draft board in Oklahoma to undergo a pre-induction physical. When completed, he was given a medical deferment and classified 4-F, unfit for military service. Osteomyelitis was one medical condition the military wanted no part of. Given that the disease involved a "long bone" and could flare up at any time, the army was not about to get stuck paying a soldier hundreds of thousands of dollars in pension payments and medical bills.

Mantle would be tested twice more by various draft boards to make sure he still warranted a 4-F deferment. The verdict was always the same; he did not qualify to fight for his country.

Still, many fans, the public in general, and some sportswriters could not understand how a player like Mantle, who was putting on such hitting and running displays in the ballpark, could not carry a gun, fly a plane, or in other ways defend America. "So Mantle has osteomyelitis," one sports columnist noted, as reported in *The Mick*. "What's the big deal? He doesn't have to *kick* anybody in Korea."

In 1951, as Mantle began his playing days with the Yankees, hate mail began to fill his mailbox. "Well, I could understand how some people felt, especially those who resented seeing young, apparently healthy guys hitting baseballs, while their own sons and husbands were being killed in battle," Mantle observed later, as noted in *Mickey Mantle: America's Prodigal Son*.

Still, the hate letters came, to say nothing of the venom tossed at him in the stadiums. "Bum," "draft dodger," and "coward" were just a few of the more polite terms to assault Mickey Mantle in his first years in the Bigs.

FOUR-SEWER MAN

New York, New York! Mantle, the hayseed, the country bumpkin, had, in April 1951, arrived. In his first year with the Yankees, the big, bad city would overwhelm him.

"In New York I lived at the Concourse Plaza Hotel, which seemed to me the ultimate in luxury," the rookie remembered in *Mickey Mantle: The Education of a Baseball Player*. "I blush sometimes to think of what I must have looked like to them, with my cardboard suitcase. . . . I had just one suit. . . . I had one pair of shoes. . . . Gradually, with the help of men like Hank Bauer, I came to understand that there was almost as much to learn about how to act off the diamond as there was about what to do when you were on."

With little to do in the evenings, Mantle would sometimes head off down the street from his hotel and play a little stickball with the locals. It was basically a game of seeing how far you could hit the ball. Distance was measured in how many manhole covers (sewers), placed 90 feet (27 meters) apart, one could span. A two-and-a-half-sewer guy was considered a local sensation. One day, Mantle smacked a ball that arched the distance of four manhole covers. Word spread fast; Mickey Mantle was a four-sewer man.

On the field, in spite of, or maybe because of, all the hype given him, Mantle got off to a slow start. By the end of April, fans still had not seen one home run. Then there were the strikeouts. Mantle would swing at anything, always going for the long ball. The results were a disaster.

In a doubleheader against Boston, Mantle struck out three times in the opener and fanned twice more in the second game. That was five strikeouts in a row. Stengel signaled to third baseman Cliff Mapes. "Get in there for Mantle," he yelled, as noted in *The Mick.* "We need somebody who can hit the ball."

The weeks dragged on and finally the moment of truth arrived. On June 15, Stengel called Mantle into his little cubbyhole. With tears in his eyes, the manager said, as recalled in *The Mick*: "This is going to hurt me more than you. . . . You're 19, that's all. I want you to get your confidence back, so I'm shipping you down to Kansas City."

Mantle would recall later, in *Mickey Mantle: The Education of a Baseball Player,* "He might as well have told me he was shipping me back to Independence. I had been a Yankee, and now I was nothing. . . . The trip to Minneapolis [where Kansas City was playing a series] was mercifully short, but I remember none of it. I was too choked up to tell anyone good-bye and too blind with misery to take any note of the passing scenery."

3

Fear Factor

Fear, depressing and uncontrollable, now gripped Mickey Mantle—the fear of failure. Though the Kansas City Blues were a Class AAA team (one step below the majors), being sent down was a demotion, with no guarantee of a return to the majors. What would his father say? What would the folks in Commerce think? Was it to be back to the mines to toil the rest of his working life deep in a hole, below the fields of play he loved so much?

At first, Mantle had a momentary resurgence of hope, as he told himself that, in his first AAA game, he would drag bunt to prove he could get on base anytime he wanted. Successful as the bunt was, manager George Selkirk was not pleased. "They didn't send you down here to bunt!" he growled, as noted in *The Mick*. "They sent you down here to hit, to get your confidence back!"

Confidence was slow in coming. "That finished me," Mantle recalled, in his 1967 autobiography. "I could feel the tears of self-pity stinging my eyes." The next 22 times at bat, Mantle went 0-for-22, not a single hit. "Whatever I had had, I told myself, I had lost it now and my baseball career was over."

Mantle called his father and told him he was quitting. He asked that he come and get him, come and take him home.

Mutt made the trip from Commerce to Kansas City, to the Aladdin Hotel where Mickey was staying, in a record five hours.

"If that's the way you're going to take this," Mutt yelled at his son, as quoted in *Mickey Mantle: The Education of a Baseball Player*, "you don't belong in baseball anyway. . . . Now you shut up! I don't want to hear that whining! I thought I raised a man, not a coward!"

The lecture worked. "That, I think, was the greatest thing my father ever did for me," Mantle recalled in his 1967 autobiography. "All the encouragement he had given me when I was small, all the sacrifices he had made so I could play ball when other boys were working in the mines, all the painstaking instruction he had provided—all these would have been thrown away if he had not been there that night to put the iron into my spine when it was needed most."

The next day Mantle hit a double, a triple, and two home runs. During the following 40 games, he went wild, with 11 home runs and 50 RBIs. Mantle's batting average reached .361. On August 14, 1951, Casey Stengel recalled Mantle to the Yankees.

MAN ABOUT TOWN

When Mantle returned to the field as a Yankee, he no longer wore No. 6 on his jersey, the number issued to him back at the beginning of the season. Assigning him that number, it was now felt, had been a mistake. Babe Ruth had been No. 3, Lou Gehrig, No. 4, and Joe DiMaggio, No. 5. Talk about pressure!

Nineteen-year-old Mantle was now given No. 7, the number that would come to define him.

Mantle was also given a roommate, actually, two roommates. Having succumbed to some shady endorsement deals earlier in the season, which the Yankees' management bailed him out of, it was felt that the naive "green-pea kid," as rookies were called in baseball, needed some "adult supervision." Hank Bauer and Johnny Hopp invited Mantle to share their apartment above the Stage Delicatessen in the White Light District of New York.

In the first game upon his return to the Yankee lineup, Mantle hit a home run. A week later, in a game his family attended, Mantle hit another homer. In the remaining 37 games he played in the 1951 season, Mantle hit .283, driving in 20 runs. No doubt about it, "The Sweet Switcher," a nickname now given him by an admiring sportswriter, had helped his team to its third straight pennant.

Off the field, Mantle was learning his way about town, getting a feel for his new "place of business," as he would always call New York City. Mantle was getting an education.

"You know in this great big city," Tommy Henrich, the team's right fielder said, as noted in *Mickey Mantle: America's Prodigal Son*, "just base hits won't do the job. Heck, baseball is a form of education. . . . Mickey'll acquire a lot of culture out of baseball. An overall polish."

To that end, Hank Bauer took Mantle shopping, to get him out of jeans and into a New York, man-about-town style. "Mickey bought two suits, two sport jackets, two pairs of slacks, two pairs of shoes and a half-dozen pairs of argyle socks," according to the *New York Times* report. Everything the young Mantle did, it seemed, was news.

THE ROOKIE TREATMENT

Mantle's first year in the majors would be his idol Joe DiMaggio's last year. The two had a strange "working" relationship, one built on both praise and resentment. Referring to his arrival with the Yankees, Mantle recalled in his book *My Favorite Summer 1956*, "I was so shy in those days and in awe when I walked into the clubhouse and looked around and saw all those big stars sitting there. Especially DiMaggio. He'd be sitting in front of his locker, drinking a cup of coffee. I couldn't believe I was in the same room with him, much less on the same team."

Did DiMaggio resent the presence of his replacement-to-be, all the talk of the next DiMaggio, even before the Yankee

☆ ☆ ☆ ☆ ☆

TOOTS SHOR'S RESTAURANT: NEW YORK'S HOT SPOT TO THE STARS

You name them, they were there: Joe DiMaggio, Frank Sinatra, Jackie Gleason, Jack Dempsey, Dwight Eisenhower, Frank Gifford, Walter Cronkite, Yogi Berra, Jimmy Hoffa, and, yes, by all means, Mickey Mantle. In fact, the Mick was one of Toots Shor's "crumbums," select friends he really liked. In the 1940s and 1950s, celebrities by the score were welcomed at the "in" spot in town, Shor's restaurant and saloon to the stars.

Located at 51 West 51st Street in Manhattan, Toots Shor's served standard American fare, such as steak, baked potato, and shrimp cocktail. The food was considered so-so, but it wasn't the food, or even the drinks, that attracted the famous—it was the chance to see and be seen. That, and to carouse with the famous proprietor himself. "Toots Shor cultivated his celebrity following by giving them unqualified admiration, loyal friendship, and a kind of happy, boozy, old-fashioned male privacy," according to the entry on Shor on the Wikipedia Web site.

DiMaggio was a favorite with Toots. Shor always ensured that DiMaggio got first-rate service without being hassled or

Clipper had a chance to exit the field gracefully? On the surface, not at all. "Why should I resent him?" DiMaggio declared in the spring of 1951, as quoted in *Mickey Mantle: America's Prodigal Son.* "If he's good enough to take my job in center, I can always move over to right or left." The great Yankee went on to say, "I haven't helped him much—Henrich takes care of that—but if there is anything I can do to help him, I'm only too willing."

For his part, Mantle would remember a relationship that never would be close. "The odd thing is, I hardly knew

☆ ☆ ☆ ☆ ☆

asked for autographs by members of the restaurant staff, other patrons, or fans. Toots courted writers, baseball executives, and especially baseball players, but there was room for all. The rich and famous, as well as the fan and the unknown, would rub elbows at the bar.

As New York changed, Shor found himself and his restaurant out of favor. With two of the city's three major-league baseball teams fleeing town in the late 1950s, with folks heading for the suburbs, and with the advent of television, the watering hole took a dive. The restaurant closed in 1971. Shor died in 1977, penniless.

Yet Shor's memory and what he meant for the nightlife of New York live on. Upon his death, the *New York Times* declared, "In a very unique manner, Toots Shor for several decades was the mirror of a special excitement and quality that set New York apart from all other cities." Much of that excitement is documented in a recently released film, *Toots Shor: Bigger Than Life.*

the man," he recalled in *The Mick*. "He was a loner, always restrained, often secretive. . . . Press me further and I'll also admit that DiMaggio never said to me, 'Come on, kid, let's have a beer and talk.'"

If Joe DiMaggio did not show resentment toward Mickey Mantle, the fans did. The booing began early in the season and never let up, continuing after his return from the minor leagues. Hank Bauer laid it on the line for Mantle. "In New York, most of the fans here are DiMaggio fans, so you're surely gonna get booed for being the guy who's gonna take his place," he said in *Mickey Mantle: America's Prodigal Son*. "It's just a New York thing."

For Mantle, the boos were hard to take. "I don't care who you are, you hear those boos," he recalled, as reported in Castro's biography. "I well understood that my being made into a rival of Joe DiMaggio turned plenty of fans against me. But I was not ready for the dirty names or the screaming profanity or the tireless abuse [of the New York fans]."

DiMaggio, as would be expected, wanted to exit on his own terms.

LOVE AND MARRIAGE

Part of Mantle's "introduction" to New York was a pretty showgirl named Holly Brooke. "Once in a while when the team was in New York and I had the evening free after a day game, we'd go out for dinner or Holly would hang out with me at the apartment on Seventh Avenue," he confessed in *The Mick*. "I guess I developed my first taste of the high life then."

The problem was that Mantle had a girlfriend back home, a girl he was actually engaged to. Merlyn Johnson had been a majorette at nearby Picher High School and a grade behind Mantle. They had started dating in his senior year. "I met the cutest little thing in Picher tonight," Mickey informed his mother (as quoted in Castro's biography) after spotting the girl at a football game. "She twirls one of the batons for the

Mickey Mantle and Merlyn Johnson, his girlfriend, are shown before a game in April 1951. Mickey and Merlyn, who had started dating during his senior year in high school, were married that December.

Picher band. She's got freckles, reddish hair, and is no taller than that."

When Mantle went off to play for the Yankees, he wrote to his high school sweetheart often, confessing his love on more than one occasion and hinting at a marriage to come. "Honey I was just trying to go to sleep but I was thinking about you so much that I thought I would just get up and write you a letter to tell you how much I miss you," he said in a letter dated May 9. "Darling I love you so much I will never be able to tell you how much but I hope in some way you will find out how much I love and miss you."

The feelings were mutual. "I developed an instant crush on Mickey Mantle," Merlyn recalled years later, as noted in *The Mick*, "and by our second or third date, I was in love with him and always would be."

But there was Holly Brooke. Mickey decided to introduce her to his father, hoping for some kind of approval. He received the opposite, as Mutt immediately pulled his son aside. "Mickey, you do the right thing and marry your own kind," he ordered his son, as declared in *Mickey Mantle: America's Prodigal Son*. "Merlyn's a sweet girl, and she's in love with you. She's what you need to keep your head straight."

Ever the dutiful son, Mickey married Merlyn on December 23, 1951, at the home of Merlyn's parents in Picher, Oklahoma. They would use Mickey's World Series bonus, practically equivalent to his year's salary, to get their marriage off to a good start.

POP GOES THE KNEE

Mantle played right field as the World Series began, with the Yankees taking on their crosstown rivals, the New York Giants. Referring to DiMaggio, Stengel told Mantle before Game 1, as reported in *Mickey Mantle: Stories & Memorabilia from a Lifetime with the Mick*: "Take everything you can get over in center, [DiMaggio's] heel is hurting pretty bad."

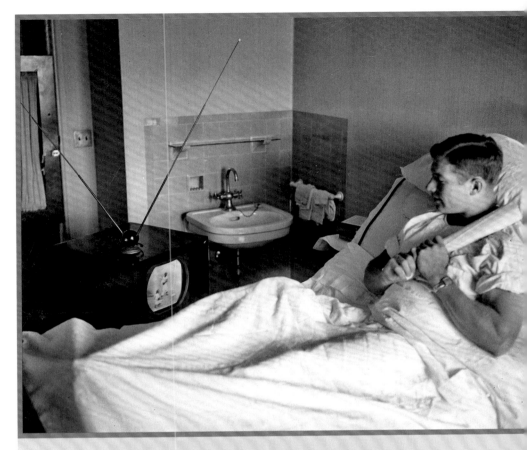

After fracturing his kneecap in the second game of the World Series, Mickey Mantle watched Game 3 from his hospital bed in New York City in October 1951. Mantle's father was hospitalized in the same room with him, having been diagnosed with cancer.

Mantle went hitless in the first game, though he did walk twice.

He would never finish the second game.

Willie Mays led off the sixth inning with a fly ball to the outfield. It was in DiMaggio's territory, but Mantle made a run for it, remembering Stengel's admonishment before the Series started. Then DiMaggio cried out, "I got it." Mantle, not wanting to plow into his idol, pulled up short. As he did, his spikes caught on the rubber cover of a drain hole. He went down as if shot, the sound actually being heard in the stands. Mantle had fractured his kneecap. The bone was sticking out of his skin. Blood was soaking his uniform. "I really thought my leg had fallen off at the knee," Mantle said.

"They're bringing out the stretcher right now," DiMaggio told Mantle, as he leaned over his fallen teammate. Mickey was carried off the field, Mutt Mantle watching from the stands.

The next morning, father and son taxied to the hospital, where Mickey was to be X-rayed. "I had to slide out of the cab and try to maneuver my good leg," Mickey recalled in *Mickey Mantle: The Education of a Baseball Player*. "My father got out first and reached in to steady me. Once on the sidewalk, I put my arm around his iron shoulders and leaned all my weight on him. Without a sound he crumpled right to the sidewalk beneath my weight."

Both Mickey and Mutt were admitted to the hospital. They wound up sharing a room and watching the rest of the World Series on a 13-inch, black-and-white television set.

With care and a physical-rehabilitation regimen, often poorly attended to by Mickey, the "Yankee Bomber" got better, though he would never play another game without pain. Mutt did not. "Your father has cancer," the doctors told Mickey, as reported in *The Mick*. "It's Hodgkin's disease. I'm afraid there's not much we can do." Mutt, the most important man in Mickey Mantle's life, was dying.

Hits and Misses

In the early spring of 1952, Joe DiMaggio, the Yankee Clipper, possibly the most revered athlete of all time, retired from baseball. If Mickey Mantle was not exactly DiMaggio's rival, he was now his idol's replacement—or so he hoped. "Losin' Joe is a tree-mendous blow," Stengel said, as reported in the *New York Times*, "but I'll still have the best outfield in the American League."

But with what players, and where would they play?

"That spring I went down to St. Petersburg, where the big question was DiMaggio's replacement in center field," Mantle recalled in *The Mick*. "I had no idea who it would be, not with me still hobbling around."

Mantle's challenger for the coveted position was Jackie Jensen. "Mantle and Jensen are quite similar in many respects," the *New York Times* reported on March 21. "They're fleet enough to cover acres of ground and blessed with powerful arms."

Although there is little doubt that Stengel favored Mantle, the young slugger still had much to learn about playing the outfield: right, left, or center. Referring to the previous season, Mantle declared, in a *New York Times* article, "My main fielding weakness was line drives hit right at me. It's still my weakness, 'cause they're tough even for a DiMaggio. There's no way of judging how deep they are, particularly if you lose them—as you usually do—against that grandstand background."

Through early May, Mantle continued to play right field. Although his thoughts were on a move to center field, he was also consumed with what was happening to his father. On May 6, while getting dressed to go to the ballpark, Mantle got a call from his manager. "I'm at the Stadium," Stengel said, as quoted in *Mickey Mantle: America's Prodigal Son.* "Your mother called here looking for you. It's your father, son. He's passed." Mutt was 39 years old.

"He never complained, he never acted scared, and he died like a man," Mantle would say years later, in his 1967 autobiography. "He didn't die scared, and he didn't live scared."

Mantle was devastated and, in the days following the death, at times inconsolable. He was racked with guilt. "So many chances then to let him know how much I loved him—and I never said it, not once," he would mournfully recall.

On May 20, in a game against Cleveland, Stengel, without telling Mantle, made out a lineup card that had the 20-year-old batting third and playing center field. Though it would not become official until June 15, the Yankees had found their successor to Joe DiMaggio. Mickey Mantle was in center field to stay.

MUMMY LEGS

In a game against the Red Sox on May 24, Mantle pulled a muscle in his left leg, forcing him to retire after only four

Because of recurring injuries, Mickey Mantle, shown here in 1965, had to wrap his legs in bandages before every game. This daily ritual began in the 1952 season and continued throughout his career.

innings of play. He would need treatment consisting of whirl-pool baths, diathermy (generating heat in the tissues by electric currents), and sessions with a machine that supplements manual massage. Such injuries, and taking the steps necessary to combat and deal with them, would now become an ongoing Mantle torment.

On virtually every game day, Mantle would begin by ritualistically wrapping both legs from his ankles to mid-thigh. His teammates would call it "mummifying," referring to how the Egyptian pharaohs were encased after death. Such observations

★ ☆ ★ ☆ ★ ☆

THE YANKEES AND THE WORLD SERIES

"I suppose it's human nature, but the Yankees of my era looked on the World Series as kind of a birthright," Mickey Mantle said, as reported in his 1967 autobiography. He had every reason to believe that.

Since 1921, when the Bronx Bombers won their first pennant, the team has played in 39 of 85 Series, winning 26. That averages to nearly a visit every other year and a title every third year. Below is a listing of the years in which the Yankees played in a World Series, with their wins highlighted in green:

1921, 1922, 1923, 1926, 1927, 1928, 1932, 1936, 1937, 1938, 1939, 1941, 1942, 1943, 1947, 1949, 1950, 1951, 1952, 1953, 1955, 1956, 1957, 1958, 1960, 1961, 1962, 1963, 1964, 1976, 1977, 1978, 1981, 1996, 1998, 1999, 2000, 2001, 2003

Mickey Mantle played in 12 World Series. Following are his World Series stats:

Year	Opponent	G	AB	H	HR	RBI	BA
1951	New York (N)	2	5	1	0	0	.200
1952	Brooklyn	7	29	10	2	3	.345

were not made in jest, however, but in reverence for the effort required. Early Wynn, the Cleveland Indians pitcher, recalled seeing Mantle go through the ritual at the 1952 All-Star Game. "I watched him bandage that knee—that whole leg—and I saw what he had to go through every day to play," Wynn recalled, as reported in Castro's biography. "He was taped from shin

★ ☆ ☆ ☆ ☆ ☆

1953	Brooklyn	6	24	5	2	7	.208
1955	Brooklyn	3	10	2	1	1	.200
1956	Brooklyn	7	24	6	3	4	.250
1957	Milwaukee	6	19	5	1	2	.263
1958	Milwaukee	7	24	6	2	3	.250
1960	Pittsburgh	7	25	10	3	11	.400
1961	Cincinnati	2	6	1	0	0	.167
1962	San Francisco	7	25	3	0	0	.120
1963	Los Angeles	4	15	2	1	1	.133
1964	St. Louis	7	24	8	3	8	.333
Totals		65	230	59	18	40	.257

Here, according to the *Baseball Reference* Web site, is a list of lifetime World Series records held by Mantle:

Most runs—42

Most runs batted in—40

Most home runs—18

Most bases on balls—43

Most strikeouts—54

Most total bases—123

Most extra-base hits—26

to thigh. And now I'll never be able to say enough in praise. Seeing those legs, his power becomes unbelievable."

Still, injuries and all, Mantle finished regular-season play with an impressive record, despite leading the league in strike-outs, with 111. He played in 142 games, had a batting average of .311, drove in 87 runs, and had 171 hits—including 37 doubles, 7 triples, and 23 home runs.

Two of those homers were grand slams, hit within a four-day period.

All of that, to be sure, was for the regular season. As personally disappointing as the 1951 World Series was for Mantle, the 1952 Series, one of a dozen he would play in, would turn out to be one of his best ever.

MR. OCTOBER

It was a crosstown rivalry like no other: the New York Yankees and the Brooklyn Dodgers. When the two teams played in a World Series, as they would in four of the next five seasons starting in 1952, they often called it a Subway Series. Before the Dodgers skipped town for good, one did not have to travel far to get from Yankee Stadium in the Bronx to Ebbets Field in Brooklyn, and back. Most fans took the subway.

The 1952 Series would go the distance to a seventh game. "There isn't anything in sports quite like the seventh game of a World Series," Mantle observed in his book *All My Octobers*. "Unlike the Super Bowl, it has taken you a week of games, not interviews, to get there. You roll out of bed and start over every day. You play offense and defense."

With the final game tied at 2-2 in the sixth inning, Mantle stepped to the plate with one out and the bases empty. Joe Black for the Dodgers was on the mound. "Black threw me a slider, I think, and I got all of it," Mantle recalled in *All My Octobers*. "The ball soared high and deep, over the scoreboard in right field and landing on the other side of Bedford Avenue. Eyeball measurements spotted the homer at 450 feet."

A Yankees batboy greeted Mickey Mantle at home plate after Mantle's sixth-inning solo home run in Game 7 of the 1952 World Series. In the next inning, he batted in a run, leading the Yankees to a 4-2 victory and the series title over the Brooklyn Dodgers.

If Mantle's homer did not win the game, it was a contributing factor. "The homer was my second in two games, and I knew this one might decide the game and the Series," he remembered in *All My Octobers*. "I tried not to show how excited I was, I kept my head down, but I think that was the fastest I ever ran around the bases. An inning later, I singled in the final run."

In a memorable post-game "encounter," Jackie Robinson of the Dodgers came to the Yankee clubhouse, specifically to shake hands with Mickey Mantle. "You're a helluva ballplayer and you've got a great future," he told the slugger, as recalled in *All My Octobers*. Mantle was stunned. "I thought that was a classy gesture, one I wasn't then capable of making," Mantle revealed. "I was a bad loser." He went on to note, "What meant even more was what Jackie told the press: 'Mantle beat us. He was the difference between the two teams. They didn't miss DiMaggio.'"

Back in Commerce, Oklahoma, they waited for their returning hero with open arms. "Mickey Mantle, one of Major League Baseball's newest and brightest stars, is going to get all the plaudits his hometown can bestow at an all-day celebration Friday," the *New York Times* announced on October 15. "He will be honored with a business district parade in the morning and a dinner in the evening." It was the first of what would be many more "Mickey Mantle Days" to come.

TAPE-MEASURE HOME RUN

Mickey Mantle was a party animal. And getting married in December 1951 seemed to have done little to slow him down in that regard. Mantle, Billy Martin, and Whitey Ford formed a famous, or infamous, trio dubbed "The Three Musketeers," men about town. "Don't get the idea that it was always party, party, party with Billy and me," Mantle said in *My Favorite Summer 1956*. "We did our share, but we had quiet times, too.

We liked to have fun, but that didn't always mean going out and drinking."

Perhaps! But as the 1953 season rolled on, Mantle observed, "By now I was no longer a hayseed from Oklahoma. I knew my way around New York, and I enjoyed taking advantage of what New York had to offer. I'm not talking about museums, art galleries, and theaters. I mean restaurants, bars, and clubs."

In an exhibition game in Brooklyn on April 15, a thunderous announcement was made over the public-address system, as recorded in *The Mick*. It should have rained on Mantle's nightlife a bit. "Ladies and gentlemen . . . now hitting . . . number seven . . . Mickey Mantle. Mickey doesn't know it yet, but he just became a father of an 8-pound, 12-ounce baby boy." It would be a month before Mantle actually saw his son, named Mickey Elvin Mantle, the middle name for his honored father.

The 1953 season for Mickey Mantle boiled down to one storied highlight that was history-making the moment it happened. On April 17, Mantle hit his first home run of the season at Griffith Stadium in Washington, D.C. It was no ordinary homer, however. "Batting right-handed, Mickey blasted the ball toward left center, where the base of the front bleachers wall is 391 feet from the plate," the *New York Times* reported. "The distance to the back of the wall is 69 feet more, and then the back wall is 50 feet high."

The ball was to sail 565 feet (172 meters) and is considered one of the longest home runs ever blasted in the majors. Reportedly, Red Patterson, the Yankees' famed publicity director, jumped from his seat and shouted, as recorded in Castro's biography, "This one has got to be measured." Thus the term "tape-measure home run" entered the lexicon.

The problem was that Patterson never had a tape measure on hand to do any measuring. As the story goes, he paced off the distance from where the ball landed to the outside bleacher wall and came up with 105 feet (32 meters). He then added the

Following a game on April 17, 1953, Mickey Mantle held up the ball he hit 565 feet, as the story goes, for a home run against the Washington Senators. After the blast, the term "tape-measure home run" was coined.

distances from home plate to the outfield wall, and from the fence to the rear wall, and arrived at a total of 565 feet.

Years later, Patterson admitted, as recalled in *Our Mickey*, "I left the press box, walked down the ramp, bought myself a hot dog and a beer, stayed in the stands about 15 minutes, and came back to announce, 'The ball went 565 feet.' Who could challenge it?"

STRAIGHT FOR THE BAR

In 1954, Mickey Mantle hit more home runs than ever before—27—and topped 100 RBIs at 102, finishing the season with an even .300 batting average. And he led the league in strikeouts again, with 107.

Yet the Indians took the pennant in 1954, breaking a major-league record with 111 wins.

While what Mantle did in ballparks during the year continued to make news and bode well for him as a maturing player, it was what was going on off the field that showed signs of trouble. Mickey Mantle was developing a drinking problem. Mickey Mantle was becoming an alcoholic.

"That past winter of 1953–4, when Billy was with me, I fell into the routine of getting out of the house by saying we were going fishing," he confessed in *The Mick*. "Instead, we would go into Joplin, have a few drinks, and before I knew it I was drunk. I wouldn't even think about going home."

A pattern was developing, a devastating one. During the off-season, Mantle started to hang around with guys who did not have jobs. By noon on most days he could be found in a bar with them, drinking. "There's no question that it became a bad problem," Mantle remembered in *The Mick*. "I know it took a toll on Merlyn and the kids. And I'm sure it took a few years off my baseball career."

In 1955, the Yankees won the pennant. However, this was the "wait until next year" season for their opponent in the

World Series—the Dodgers. It was also the year that *Damn Yankees* became a hit musical on Broadway. The show was the saga of a baseball fan who sold his soul to the devil. The story was based on a book called *The Year the Yankees Lost the Pennant.* Though the Yankees did not lose the pennant in 1955, they did lose the World Series.

For the Dodgers, winning the Series, especially after losing the first two games, was sweet triumph indeed. Amazingly, it was their first Series victory.

For Mantle, the Yankees' Series loss was a disaster. He vowed that next year things would be different. They were. Not only would the Bronx Bombers capture the pennant and the World Series, but Mantle would finally play up to the full potential his manager, Casey Stengel, had been waiting for.

Yankee Superstar

Before 1956 I was doing pretty well," Mickey Mantle declared in *The Mick*, "but I wasn't Babe Ruth, Joe DiMaggio, and Lou Gehrig all rolled into one. That season I started to do the things they thought I would do."

True, Mantle would hit for a higher average the following year, .365. And in 1961, he would smash more home runs than he did in 1956, clobbering 54. Yet it was 1956 that saw all phases of his game come together. It would be the year that Mickey Mantle lived up to his full potential and maturity.

The record speaks for itself. Mantle would win the American League's Most Valuable Player (MVP) award. He would beat out Ted Williams for the batting championship. And the "Oklahoma Kid" would become only one of a dozen major leaguers in history to win the coveted Triple Crown,

leading with a .353 batting average, 52 home runs, and 130 RBIs. "Everything just seemed to go right for me that year," Mantle remembered in *My Favorite Summer 1956*. "The big thing was that I was healthy most of the season and everything just kind of fell into place."

Indeed, a healthy season would prove decisive in Mantle's awesome accomplishments. He had only a slightly sprained knee to slow him down. Mantle missed but four games the entire season.

Early on, even before the regular season commenced, it was apparent to many that Mantle's time had arrived. No less a competitor than Williams, the last major leaguer to hit over .400, said it best, as reported in the *New York Times* of April 22, "As far as I can see, Mickey has improved every year and he'll continue to improve. My guess is that he's now heading definitely for his peak. Why shouldn't he be great? He has good speed, good swing, and good power. There's no reason in the world why he can't be a .340 hitter and a 40-homer slugger—or better."

Better, to be sure, 1956 would turn out to be.

COMING OF AGE

President Dwight D. Eisenhower threw out the ceremonial first pitch as the Yankees opened the season against the Washington Senators, known to their detractors as "first in war, first in peace, and last in the American League," on April 17 at Griffith Stadium. Mantle stood in line with his other teammates to shake the president's hand. In the game, in which the Yankees defeated the Senators, 10-4, Mantle hit two home runs over the center-field fence that some say traveled more than 450 feet (137 meters). And he did it, it seemed, without even trying.

Given what Mantle told Arthur Daley of the *New York Times* a few days later, that may have been just what happened. "I've quit trying to hit home runs every time I go to bat," Mantle revealed. "From now on I'm just trying to keep from striking out. All I want to do is meet the ball. If I do that, I'll have a good year."

Referring to the two home runs on Opening Day, Mantle went on to say, "I didn't swing hard at either of them. I did what I've been trying to do all along—just meet the ball. If I can cut down my strikeouts and keep getting wood on the ball, enough of them will go out of the park. I can get more homers that way than I can by deliberately going for the long ball."

And those homers, indeed, kept coming. On Memorial Day, in a game against the Senators at Yankee Stadium, Mantle hit his most memorable home run of the year. The blast, had it not struck the grandstand's filigreed facade but 18 inches from the top of the Stadium roof, would have traveled 600 feet (183 meters), some estimated. Nobody has ever hit a ball out of Yankee Stadium, though Mantle's Memorial Day rocket came as close as any had.

Come midsummer and the All-Star Game, Mantle was the top vote-getter in the fan balloting. Too bad he never saw the game's significance.

"One thing I always regretted about my career is that I never took the All-Star Game seriously enough," he said in *My Favorite Summer 1956*. "I usually looked at it as a few days off to more or less rest and to party."

One thing Mantle did like about the All-Star Game, however, was his chance to be on the same team as his hero Ted Williams. In direct contrast to Mantle, Williams took the game quite seriously. For Williams, it was an opportunity to check out all the pitchers, many of whom he would be competing against the rest of the year.

Williams was more than willing to share his hitting hints with Mantle. Yet the instruction rarely took. All that technical talk was too much for Mantle, and possibly detrimental. "When I left him," Mantle recalled in *My Favorite Summer 1956*, "I started thinking about all the things he told me, and I didn't get a hit for about 25 times at bat."

CHASING THE BABE

In 1927, in a 154-game season, Babe Ruth hit 60 home runs. In 1956, the record still stood. By mid-June, the fans, the sports commentators, and even Mantle began to notice that the papers were printing the number of games Mickey was ahead of the Babe, and the writers were beginning to ask him

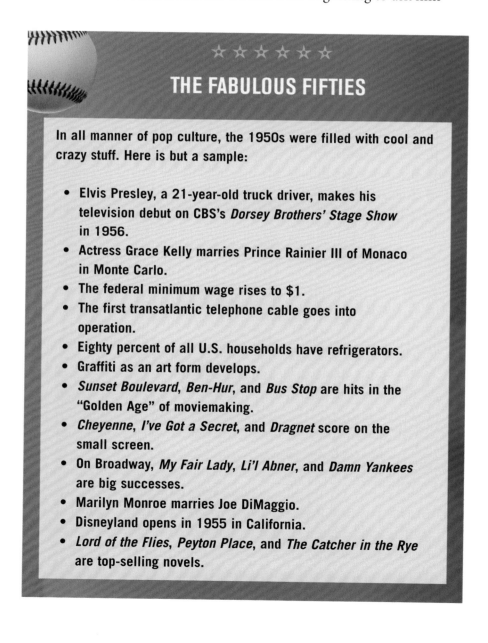

☆ ☆ ☆ ☆ ☆ ☆

THE FABULOUS FIFTIES

In all manner of pop culture, the 1950s were filled with cool and crazy stuff. Here is but a sample:

- Elvis Presley, a 21-year-old truck driver, makes his television debut on CBS's *Dorsey Brothers' Stage Show* in 1956.
- Actress Grace Kelly marries Prince Rainier III of Monaco in Monte Carlo.
- The federal minimum wage rises to $1.
- The first transatlantic telephone cable goes into operation.
- Eighty percent of all U.S. households have refrigerators.
- Graffiti as an art form develops.
- *Sunset Boulevard*, *Ben-Hur*, and *Bus Stop* are hits in the "Golden Age" of moviemaking.
- *Cheyenne*, *I've Got a Secret*, and *Dragnet* score on the small screen.
- On Broadway, *My Fair Lady*, *Li'l Abner*, and *Damn Yankees* are big successes.
- Marilyn Monroe marries Joe DiMaggio.
- Disneyland opens in 1955 in California.
- *Lord of the Flies*, *Peyton Place*, and *The Catcher in the Rye* are top-selling novels.

about breaking the record. "I just told them it was too early to think of that, and it was," Mantle responded, as noted in *My Favorite Summer 1956.*

Challenging Babe Ruth's mark had been done before, of course, to no avail.

Jimmie Foxx smashed 58 home runs in 1932.

★ ★ ★ ★ ★ ★

Mickey Mantle, to be sure, was very much a part of the decade, becoming its iconic sports character. "He had the look of sunshine: blond hair, blue eyes, freckles, that big, easy smile, an Oklahoma drawl, and a walk just short of a swagger," said Mickey Herskowitz in *Mickey Mantle: Stories & Memorabilia from a Lifetime with the Mick.* "He was every mother's son."

"I guess you could say I'm what this country's all about," Mantle famously said, and did so in all modesty. "He was all that America wanted itself to be," added Tony Castro, his main biographer, "and he was also all that America feared it could never be."

Yet for Mantle, it was not all bright skies and green lights. The "Oklahoma Kid," according to FBI files, was being threatened by gamblers and blackmailed for supposedly having an affair with a married woman. Mantle claimed neither took place.

The 1950s, for Mantle and the world at large, had their serious side, too. Civil-rights activists were marching. War broke out in the Middle East. And the Soviet Union woke the United States out of its complacency with the launch of Sputnik I, the first artificial satellite.

Still seen as an innocent decade, for many the '50s actually ended not on December 31, 1959, but on November 23, 1963, the day President John F. Kennedy was assassinated in Dallas, Texas. The new, turbulent '60s were about to begin.

The lights of Yankee Stadium shone down on Mickey Mantle, who was at the plate, during a game against the Kansas City Athletics in July 1956. Through much of the season, Mantle was keeping pace with Babe Ruth's single-season home-run record of 60.

Hank Greenberg did the same in 1938.

And Johnny Mize hit 43 homers in the 1940 season.

But all succumbed to what was known as the "September fade."

At the All-Star break, Mantle had 29 home runs, one game ahead of Ruth's pace. By the end of August, he had 47 homers. Mantle needed 13 more in 25 games to tie Ruth, 14 more to beat him. But now it was September. "A lot of guys had come into September with a chance to break the Babe's record and couldn't do it," Mantle said in *My Favorite Summer 1956*. "The year he hit 60, the Babe hit 17 in the month of September and that's what killed off all the challengers—17 homers in a month, plus all the pressure. That stopped everybody."

Mantle claimed that it never meant that much to him to beat the Babe, at least not in 1956. "I was no Babe Ruth and did not mean to be," he declared in his 1967 autobiography. What meant a lot to Mantle, more than Ruth's record, was winning the batting championship, something he had yet to do. To succeed, however, Mantle had to watch his back. Ted Williams, at age 38 and closing in on his last years in baseball, wanted the same title and just as badly.

The problem for Williams was that he was always too proud to swing at bad pitches. As a result, he would pick up a fair number of walks, none of which counted as official at-bats. As the season closed out, Williams was running out of at-bats to reach the 400 he would need to qualify for any batting title.

In the end, Williams conceded the title to Mantle, batting .345 to the "Commerce Kid's" .353. Yet Williams, the "Splendid Splinter," figured if he could run like Mantle, he would have hit .400 every year.

TRIPLE CROWN

About mid-season, it appeared that the jeers the Yankees were used to receiving whenever they played out of town were, miraculously, turning into cheers. "A remarkable change seems to have come over baseball fans," wrote Louis Effrat in the *New York Times* on June 26. "Those who used to jeer the all-conquering Yankees now are cheering Casey Stengel's Bombers." It happened everywhere the Yanks went, so much so that playing out of town was not much different from playing at home.

Of course, the reason for the Yankees' new appeal rested with one man—Mickey Mantle. When Mantle played, the cheers went up. In one incident, at Briggs Stadium in Detroit, after Mantle hit his twenty-seventh home run, the outfield sprinkler system had to be turned on to save him from being mobbed.

No doubt about it, as Mantle's "dream season" pressed on, the "Switch-Hitting Slugger" became the most-talked-about player in baseball. He appeared on the covers of national magazines and on numerous television shows. Mantle was instantly recognized everywhere he went. While enjoying the limelight, he seemed to take the adulation in stride.

Besides winning the batting title in 1956, Mantle also took the year's MVP award, the first of three he would receive. That left only one more prize, the most coveted—the Triple Crown. Mantle had the batting title with .353. The home-run honor had been cinched with 52 homers, 20 more than the runner-up, Vic Wertz of the Indians. It was the RBI category that Mantle had to sweat out, practically to the last day. Mantle's RBI total stood at 130. But Detroit's Al Kaline, going into his final game, had 126. Anxiously, Mantle waited for word from Detroit. It came—Kaline had driven in only two runs. Mickey Mantle had won the Triple Crown.

Yet as terrific as the season had been for Mantle, with all the accomplishments and all the titles, the slugger claimed it would have meant nothing, it would have all been a waste, had the Yankees not been given a chance to beat the Dodgers in a World Series rematch. Revenge time was at hand.

Saving Don Larsen's perfect game, Mickey Mantle (No. 7) ran down a deep fly ball hit into left center by the Brooklyn Dodgers' Gil Hodges in the fifth inning of Game 5 of the 1956 World Series. "It was the best catch I ever made," Mantle said. The Yankees defeated their crosstown rivals, but they needed all seven games to win the World Series.

WORLD SERIES RETALIATION

The Yankees hated to lose a World Series. Even though they had won four out of five over the years against their crosstown rivals, in 1956 they were out to avenge the defeat of the previous season.

The Yankees would do just that, but it would take seven games. And they would have to fend off a comeback from the

Dodgers in the sixth game, determined as they were to crawl out from under the most humiliating defeat in World Series history. It would be a fifth game in which not a single Dodger made it to first base. Twenty-seven Dodgers would swing a bat; twenty-seven Dodgers would be called out. In other words, the Yankees would deliver a perfect game.

The Dodgers took the first two games at Ebbets Field, and the Yanks the second two in their own Stadium. Going into the fifth game at the Yankees' ballpark, the Bronx Bombers gave "Goony Bird," pitcher Don Larsen, the start. Known as a party boy second only to Mantle himself, Larsen nonetheless stayed sober throughout the Series. Good thing, too.

In the top of the fifth inning, Gil Hodges of the Dodgers came to bat. The boys from Brooklyn still had not produced a single hit. On a 2-2 count, Hodges drove a line drive into left center. "I ran like hell," Mantle remembered in *My Favorite Summer 1956.* "I just put my head down and took off as fast as I could. I caught up with the ball as it was dropping, more than 400 feet from home plate."

Mantle went on to declare, "It was the best catch I ever made. Some people might question that, but there's certainly no question that it was the most *important* catch I ever made."

Indeed! If Mantle had muffed that grab, there is little doubt the ball would have dropped for at least a double. For a pitcher to pitch a perfect game, he needs not only incredible ball control, but he also needs the help of every teammate in the field. That day, he got Mantle's.

There have been about 200 no-hitters in the history of major-league play. There have been but 15 perfect games. And there has been only one such game in a World Series, the fifth game of the 1956 Fall Classic.

The Dodgers, to their credit, picked up the pieces and came back to win the sixth game. The Yankees, though, put it away in the seventh contest. A perfect ending to a perfect season. Mickey Mantle's favorite summer.

A Rookie
No More

Thanks to many of his fun-loving teammates (particularly Whitey Ford and Billy Martin), Mickey Mantle discovered soon enough that New York City had attractions that a small town like Commerce, Oklahoma, never did. On May 15, 1957, a half-dozen Yankees, along with most of their wives, chose to celebrate Martin's twenty-ninth birthday at one of the hottest spots in Manhattan, the famed Copacabana nightclub. It would have been better had they all stayed home.

Actually, the party began with dinner at Danny's Hideaway, then continued at the Waldorf Astoria hotel, and wound up at the Copa, where Sammy Davis, Jr., was on stage. Also at the show was a 220-pound (100-kilogram) Yankee fan named Edward Jones and his party, numbering 17, celebrating the end of the bowling season.

Sometime around 2:30 A.M., the bowlers began to heckle Davis, making crude references like "Little Black Sambo" and "Jungle Bunny." The Yankees tried to quiet the Jones party down, to no avail. Soon enough, all hell broke loose, as the players' wives were hastily ushered out of the nightclub. Jones claims he was hit in the face by Hank Bauer and suffered a fractured nose and jaw. Bauer, who had been hitting .203 for the season, denied the charge, declaring (in Castro's biography), "Hit him? Why I haven't hit anybody all year."

Lawyers were retained. A grand jury was called. And the players were summoned to testify. When Yogi Berra proclaimed, "Nobody did nothin' to nobody," the jury broke out laughing, and an hour later the district attorney threw out the case for insufficient evidence.

That was not the end of it, however. George Weiss, the Yankees' general manager, fined the bunch a total of $5,100. The incident would give Weiss the excuse he needed to eventually trade Billy Martin to Kansas City.

"I was only 25 years old, getting a little cocky—also grossing up to about $75,000 in outside income and figuring there was no telling how much I would make by the time I was 30," Mantle confessed in *The Mick*. Reflecting on his family history with Hodgkin's disease, when many in his father's generation were not living into their 40s, Mantle saw reason enough to live it up while he could.

ALL-AMERICAN BOY

Mantle, indeed, was making good money the year after winning the Triple Crown. In 1957, he signed a contract for $60,000. Endorsements were bringing in that and more. Celebrating their new wealth, the Mantles bought a four-bedroom home in the fashionable Preston Hollow section of Dallas, Texas, for $59,500 the previous year.

Although the Yankees lost the 1957 World Series, as the Milwaukee Braves beat them in seven games, Mantle still took home the American League MVP award, his second. In 1958, Mantle signed for $70,000. He had become one of the highest-paid athletes in the nation.

The Braves had, of course, been the Boston Braves until 1953. From 1903 to that year, a half-century, not a single major-league ball club left its hometown. The Braves' move to Milwaukee opened the way for other teams to flee, notably the New York ball clubs, the Dodgers and the Giants, which headed west to Los Angeles and San Francisco, respectively, in 1958.

With the Big Apple now all to themselves, the Yankees bounced back in the 1958 Fall Classic, reversing the previous year's fortunes by beating the Braves, four games to three. Despite recurring injuries to his right knee and his shoulder, Mantle had a good year, batting .304, hitting 42 home runs, and chalking up an RBI total of 97. Always out to win, Mantle declared in *All My Octobers*, "No matter how much money you make, or how much fame you fall into, if you consider yourself a competitor, you don't like to lose. You don't like to be embarrassed."

The late 1950s saw not only the expansion west of baseball, but, not unrelated, the explosion of television viewership. While shows like *I Love Lucy*, *Cheyenne*, and *The Mickey Mouse Club* were drawing millions to the small screen every week, so, too, was sport, particularly baseball. And who better to personify the American pastime, with his famous swing and rocket speed, than Mickey Mantle? Already an East Coast celebrity, television made Mantle a national icon, an All-American boy.

Off the screen, however, the images of Mantle were more sobering, figuratively though not literally. His marriage was showing real strain.

The telling moment came on December 5, 1957, with the birth of the Mantles' third son, Billy, named after Billy Martin. As Merlyn checked herself into a hospital in Joplin, Missouri, to deliver, Mantle was out hunting in Texas with the boys. He was flown back to his wife's bedside in a private plane. Merlyn simply lamented, as reported in Tony Castro's biography, "You could've waited a few more days before taking off like that!"

BOOING AND JEERING

With the Yankees the only game in town and Mantle the only real star, expectations for the "Oklahoma Kid" were running

☆ ☆ ☆ ☆ ☆ ☆

MAJOR-LEAGUE EXPANSION

When the Boston Braves became the Milwaukee Braves in 1953, it wasn't expansion, it was movement. Major-league teams that had been anchored to their hometowns for 50 years were starting to pick up and go elsewhere. With the advent of national television in the 1950s, the pressure to expand the two major leagues, the American and the National, beyond eight teams each became unstoppable. Other cities wanted to play the big boy's game. They wanted major-league action, too.

The American League was the first to add teams: two in 1961, the Los Angeles Angels (now of Anaheim) and the Washington Senators (now the Texas Rangers). (That same year, the original Washington Senators had moved to Minnesota.)

The following year, the National League took on two new teams: the Houston Colt .45s (now the Astros) and the New York Mets.

In 1969, both leagues went to 12 teams and split into two divisions. By 1993, the two leagues had 14 teams apiece. Today, the American League has 14 teams in three divisions; the National League has 16 teams, also in three divisions. The breakdown is as follows:

high. Fans were prepared to demonstrate that failure to perform was not an option.

Booing and catcalling baseball players were nothing new, of course. When it went beyond the verbal, however, things could get downright ugly.

In 1934, Ducky Medwick, an outfielder with the St. Louis Cardinals, was pelted with fruit by Detroit fans during the

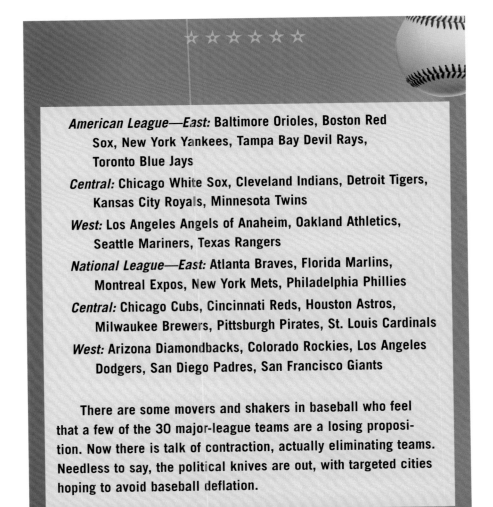

American League—East: Baltimore Orioles, Boston Red Sox, New York Yankees, Tampa Bay Devil Rays, Toronto Blue Jays

Central: Chicago White Sox, Cleveland Indians, Detroit Tigers, Kansas City Royals, Minnesota Twins

West: Los Angeles Angels of Anaheim, Oakland Athletics, Seattle Mariners, Texas Rangers

National League—East: Atlanta Braves, Florida Marlins, Montreal Expos, New York Mets, Philadelphia Phillies

Central: Chicago Cubs, Cincinnati Reds, Houston Astros, Milwaukee Brewers, Pittsburgh Pirates, St. Louis Cardinals

West: Arizona Diamondbacks, Colorado Rockies, Los Angeles Dodgers, San Diego Padres, San Francisco Giants

There are some movers and shakers in baseball who feel that a few of the 30 major-league teams are a losing proposition. Now there is talk of contraction, actually eliminating teams. Needless to say, the political knives are out, with targeted cities hoping to avoid baseball deflation.

Fans flocked toward Mickey Mantle after he hit a game-winning home run in the tenth inning against the Chicago White Sox in June 1959. Throughout much of the 1950s, fans had a love-hate relationship with Mantle. They would boo him after a strikeout. Then they would swarm him after a game-winning hit.

World Series. In 1949, Eddie Waitkus of the Phillies was shot with a pistol by a "devoted" fan. And in 1956, the Giants' Whitey Lockman had a beer bottle heaved at his skull, the missile having been broken open before taking flight.

Mantle would often get the "treatment" even before entering a ballpark. "Every time he drives up to Yankee Stadium, he is mobbed by a pack of young baseball fanatics," wrote Gay Talese, in a June 1, 1958, article for the *New York Times*. "If he does not stop to sign autographs, some teenagers squirt ink into his clothing."

The reasons for the manhandling and verbal assaults aimed at "The Hero of New York" are not hard to discern.

"We don't like Mickey," one fan declared to Talese. "He's stuck up." "Maybe it's because we expect too much from Mantle," another volunteered. "He's been getting booed since he came to the Stadium. He got too much publicity when he first came up."

And then there was the salary Mantle was making. "Anybody who gets all that money has got to deliver," said a Harlem theater manager. "In my theater, when the sound goes off, or when there's a blank screen, people stomp, whistle and holler. Me, I got no other outlet but to boo Mantle. He's got to deliver."

Yet in 1958 and 1959, Mantle was, according to many (including himself), not delivering—at least not at his 1956 level. "I'd like to forget 1959 altogether as far as baseball goes," Mantle confessed in *The Mick*. "The whole season seemed to be loaded with mishaps. . . . It was only the second time we lost the pennant in the time I had been with the team."

The Yankees finished third in the American League that year, and down with them went Mantle. "I'd sit with my head hanging, deep in the dumps, knowing I wasn't contributing as much as I wanted to," Mantle continued. "Aggravating injuries were part of it. I also worried about my hitting, worried about helping the guys I worked and played with—I worried about everything." In 1959, Mantle's average dropped below .300, to .285. Not since 1953 had he finished a season under the magic .300 mark.

A MOST UNLIKELY SERIES

For Mantle, the 1960 season would come down to one climactic World Series, upon which Mantle would reflect bitterly, in

All My Octobers, "The better team lost, the only time I truly felt that way. It wasn't even close."

To be sure, the season had its highlights for Mantle, now 28 years old and a rookie no more. Although there were still plenty of jeers, there were also cheers. The idolization had never really ceased. In fact, worship of the man, the need to get a piece of him, could not only get a bit goofy, but often-times threatening. Jim Kaat, a former pitcher and a Yankees' broadcaster for many years, recalls in the book *Our Mickey* an incident in 1960 that had become all too typical of Mantle and his relationship with the fans:

> Well, [Julio] Becquer hits a long fly ball to center, and Mickey goes back to get it. As he catches it, the fans start streaming onto the field. All of a sudden I look up and I see several thousand fans on the field, and they are all running in the same direction toward center field and toward Mickey. . . . Mickey grabs his hat and his glove and tucks them under his arm and starts running for the dugout about 400 feet away. He looked like the greatest football broken field runner, dashing and dodging among all those fans trying to touch him or steal his cap or stop him for an autograph. That was something.

The World Series saw the Pirates beat the Yankees in seven. Mantle would reflect that he had never been in a Series as wacky, a Series in which he would need to remind himself that such play is decided on games won, not on runs scored.

The Yankees outscored the Pirates 55 to 27. They out-homered them 10 to 4. And they outpitched them with Whitey Ford's two shutouts. Mantle hit three home runs, batted .400, drove in eleven runs, scored eight runs, and walked eight times. Still the Yankees lost.

For Mantle, the defeat represented the greatest ballplaying disappointment of his life. "In the locker room all of us are

The legacies of Mickey Mantle and Yankees manager Casey Stengel *(left)*, shown here in 1957, were intertwined. Stengel, who led the Yankees to seven World Series titles, was fired after the team lost the Fall Classic in 1960. "Casey had been good to me from the start," Mantle said.

wandering around in a trance, muttering, 'What happened?'" he recalled in *The Mick*. "I'm slumped on a stool, feeling so low I can hardly peel off my uniform."

When Mantle retreated to the trainer's room, he cried uncontrollably. He did the same on the plane ride home.

STENGEL TAKES A HIT

Two days after the Yankees lost the 1960 World Series, their manager lost his job—the manager who had won more Fall Classics for the team than any other in history. In Casey Stengel's first year with the Bronx Bombers, in 1949, he delivered a championship. And he kept on delivering, in 1950, '51, '52, and '53—five years in a row. Stengel would do it again in 1956 and 1958. But when he failed to come through in 1960, he was fired.

Age was given as the official front-office reason for Stengel's release—"The Old Professor" was now 70. There was more to it than that, though. The Yankees' heads wanted new management blood to work with what would obviously need to be new player blood coming up. And to be sure, the World Series loss, caused, many felt, by Stengel's strange refusal to start pitcher Whitey Ford in the opener, did not help. Stengel would claim he was saving Ford for the first game at Yankee Stadium. Still, the decision did not make sense, and the Yankees suffered because of it. Perhaps Stengel was just losing it? Maybe he just did not have it anymore?

For Mantle, Stengel's departure was bittersweet. "Casey had been good to me from the start," he said in *Mickey Mantle: The Education of a Baseball Player.* "It was he who brought me to the Yankees at least a year, and maybe two years, before the upstairs management thought I was ready, and so it was Casey who helped my father realize his dream before he died."

The relationship between the two, the great manager and the great player, had been a complex one from the beginning. Years later, in *All My Octobers*, Mantle had figured it out pretty well, though. "He wanted me to be part of his legacy to the game," Mantle said, referring to Stengel. "He wanted me to be the greatest player of all time, and he may have wanted that more than I wanted it for myself."

When voting for the league's MVP award was finalized on November 9, 1960, it showed that Mickey Mantle was still considered one of the greatest to ever swing a bat. He did not win the honor, though. A new Yankee, four years in the majors, but in his first year with the team, took home the prize—Roger Maris. In the second-closest balloting in the history of the award, Maris edged out Mantle, 225 to 222. The 24-man award committee had come closer only once before, when Joe DiMaggio beat out Ted Williams, 202 to 201, in 1947.

When it came to home runs, Maris and Mantle could not have been any tighter. Maris hit 39 in 1960, and Mantle hit 40, to lead the league. It looked like a long-ball competition in the making. Next year, with Babe Ruth's target of 60 to aim for, the striving and the rivalry would grip the world of sports.

Home-Run Derby

On January 20, 1961, the oldest man up to that time to occupy the White House, 70-year-old Dwight D. Eisenhower, shook hands with his successor, the youngest man to win the presidency—John F. Kennedy. As the new, boyish president would declare moments later in his inaugural address: "The torch has been passed to a new generation of Americans."

John F. Kennedy presented an image of youthful vigor to a nation ready to charge ahead in new directions. Scenes of the young president playing touch football with family and cabinet members soon filled television screens throughout the nation. Sport was much a part of the Kennedy tradition. As the baseball season geared up, from the lowliest fan in the bleachers to the White House occupant, all eyes were eager to see what 1961 would bring. Few would be disappointed.

For Mickey Mantle, the new season would start with an added assignment. The day that Ralph Houk, Casey Stengel's replacement, began as manager, he called Mantle into his office. "You have to be the leader of the team," he told the 29-year-old, as reported in *Our Mickey: Cherished Memories of an American Icon.* When Mantle responded, "How do I do that?" Houk simply replied, "Just be yourself. I don't want you to do anything more than keep the guys fired up by your own actions. I know you can."

Mantle responded to the honor philosophically. "Making me team leader," he recalled in *Mickey Mantle: The Education of a Baseball Player,* "suddenly took me out of myself and made me see that other people had problems and emotions. It just about put an end to my worst sulks and tantrums. I knew I was supposed to be setting the example."

Mantle was chosen for leadership because Houk knew he had the respect of his teammates. Unlike Joe DiMaggio, Mantle was one of the guys. He would unselfishly play in pain. He would help young players make the transition to the big leagues. And Mantle could lead silently by example. He may not have been the fans' darling, as DiMaggio was, but he was the players' favorite. Tom Tresh, who played with Mantle from 1961 to 1968, said it best, in *Our Mickey*, when he declared: "It was just the greatest baseball experience of a lot of lives on the Yankees to play on the same team with Mickey Mantle. We not only respected him as the game's greatest player, we loved him as a man. How did we show it? We named children after him."

THE M&M BOYS

While Mickey Mantle was celebrating a decade as a Yankee, a new teammate, Roger Maris, began his second full season with the team. A gifted athlete from Fargo, North Dakota, Maris made his major-league debut with the Cleveland Indians in

1957. The next year, he was traded to the Kansas City Athletics. In 1960, he came to the Yankees, where he led the league in slugging percentage and RBIs, and finished second behind Mantle in home runs and total bases. Though he won the American League's MVP award that year, Maris averaged but .283. Maris would never bat over .300 in his entire 12-year career.

Together in 1961, Maris and Mantle, who would soon become known as the M&M boys, hit an astonishing 115 home runs for the season. That broke the Ruth-Gehrig mark of 107, set in 1927. The two Yankees also competed, fiercely, to determine not only which one would hit the most home runs in 1961, but also, if possible, who would beat Babe Ruth's season record of 60. As spring matured into summer, fans were beginning to speculate as to whether Mantle or Maris, or both, would do "61 in '61."

Rivalry on the field, however, never extended to off-field antagonism, even though the press insisted deep tensions existed. Early in the season, Bob Cerv and Roger Maris began to share an apartment together. Later, Mantle joined them. Mantle, it seemed, was concerned about the pressure building on Maris as their home-run numbers mounted, and he wanted to help his teammate out. "I was with him practically every step of the way," Mantle remembered in *The Mick.* "I know the dues he paid to get there."

There would be plenty of stress, indeed. Mantle, a seasoned pro by now, could handle what the press demanded of him. He had learned from years on the job, in media-savvy New York, what to say and not to say. Not so with Maris. Considered a blunt-spoken upper Midwesterner, small-town Roger Maris did not know how to schmooze the media and, more to the point, did not want to know.

As a result, the press was quick to root for Mantle and belittle Maris. Furthermore, as the home-run derby intensified, many fans became upset with the prospect of anyone breaking the beloved Babe Ruth's record, least of all a "sophomore" Yankee playing in only his second year. If anyone were to surpass "The Sultan of Swat," it should be Mantle, they felt. He had earned the right to do it. Soon, the booing and jeering that in recent years had stung Mantle began to wound Maris.

RECORD RUN

On July 17, midway through the season, baseball commissioner Ford Frick announced that the addition of eight games to American League play, taking the number played from 154 to 162, was going to affect record-keeping. He ruled that, if a player were to break Ruth's record of 60 home runs, he would have to do it by smacking 61 in 154 games. If such a player surged ahead in the last eight games, a note, perhaps an asterisk, would be placed after his mark—a stain for all time.

The M&M boys paid scant attention to Frick's comment at the time, choosing to concentrate on running up round-trippers. By mid-August, the two were even, at 45 apiece. On September 2, Maris surged ahead, hitting his fifty-second and fifty-third home runs. The next day, Mantle hit two, bringing his number to 50. And so it went, with Maris remaining ahead by a few, but Mantle right on his tail. Mantle, for the first time in his career as a Yankee, was the underdog. Fans reacted with cheers for the "Oklahoma Kid." They booed the newcomer, Roger Maris.

Some felt that the boy from Fargo gained a decisive advantage when manager Houk decided early on to switch him and Mantle in the batting order. Putting Mantle fourth, in the cleanup spot, meant that Maris, now batting third, would get better pitches to hit. Opposing hurlers, it was argued, would rather pitch to Maris, not around him. A pitcher did not want

(*continues on page 73*)

☆ ☆ ☆ ☆ ☆ ☆

BASEBALL AND THE *

In 1961, as the M&M boys struggled to see who, if either, would surpass Babe Ruth's record of 60 long balls in one season, baseball commissioner Ford Frick got nervous. Having ghostwritten an autobiography of "The Babe" in his previous profession as a sportswriter, Frick had an interest in preserving as long as possible the "Sultan of Swat's" reputation for smacking them out of the park. In a blatant conflict of interest, he decreed that should Maris or Mantle surpass Ruth, they would have to accomplish the feat in 154 games to make it legitimate. When Ruth set his record in 1927, teams played 154 games. If either player, or any player for that matter, broke the record during the eight additional games the league now played, an asterisk should appear next to the player's name as a symbol of "attenuated heroism," as writer Douglas Kern called it.

In Maris's case, the asterisk was never implemented, though there are many today who scan to the bottom of a page whenever Roger Maris's name appears. For 37 years, until Mark McGwire hit 70 home runs, Maris's record stood—no scarlet asterisk attached.

Nonetheless, the asterisk, and what it symbolizes, remains a controversial issue in baseball. This is particularly true when it comes to home runs, in what is possibly the single most important individual record in professional sports. Frick and others argued at the time that Maris's 1961 challenge to Ruth was a product of baseball expansion. It was felt that (1) Maris was eligible to play in eight more games than Ruth, and (2) he would, as a result of such expansion, face weaker pitching.

☆ ☆ ☆ ☆ ☆ ☆

It is important to remember, however, that Ruth's 60-home-run season was controversial, too. There were those who maintained that the Babe was a mere smacker who could not or would not play the game as it was in the Dead Ball Era.

Frick's ruling, which included any record challenged in Games 155 through 162, made no sense. Did that mean additional hits and games won meant nothing to individual players? And what about strikeouts and errors? Should they not count, then?

"All record-setting performances are the products of their times and are frequently accomplished in unique circumstances," wrote the editors of the *2006 ESPN Baseball Encyclopedia.* "All players that set important records both enjoyed and exploited whatever significant advantages time and fate gave them."

In 1998, a new home-run derby electrified baseball fans, as Mark McGwire of the St. Louis Cardinals battled bat-to-bat with Sammy Sosa of the Chicago Cubs to see who could eclipse Maris's record. McGwire won, hitting 70 homers, though Sosa smashed 66, also surpassing Maris. With smaller ballparks and pitching staffs supposedly diluted further by more expansion, some sought to challenge the new records, for the same old reasons. In an ESPN poll conducted in February 2005, more respondents voted for Maris as the legitimate holder of the home-run record than anyone—ahead of Ruth, McGwire, and Barry Bonds, who hit 73 home runs in 2001. Go figure! Ford Frick must be spinning in his grave.

In 1961, everyone in baseball was watching the home-run battle between Yankee teammates Roger Maris *(left)* and Mickey Mantle. Despite being rivals for the record, the two men were close friends off the field and even roommates during the '61 season.

(*continued from page 69*)

to put Maris on base with Mantle coming up. Thus Maris would get fewer walks.

Interestingly, Mantle saw the switch as being to his advantage, too. "I had Roger Maris hitting in front of me, so pitchers were not 'pitching around' me—throwing me nothing but bad pitches and chancing a base on balls—the way they used to do," he said in *Mickey Mantle: The Education of a Baseball Player*. "Too often big Roger was there on first base ahead of me, and no pitcher wanted to push him to second base without charge."

With the season now into September, the pressure on Maris, the leader, proved unrelenting. He was chain-smoking Camels, up to four packs a day. His hair began to fall out in chunks. He had become a nervous wreck.

Mantle was not immune to stress, either. He was becoming run down physically. Given his after-game lifestyle, it was easy to see why. Mantle caught the flu. On a train ride from Boston, Mantle, feverish and sweating, sat next to Mel Allen, the team's announcer. Allen gave Mantle the name of a doctor. Maybe a quick shot of something would snap the flu in its tracks. It was worth a try.

SHOT IN THE HIP

Mantle arrived at Dr. Max Jacobson's office dragging. His spirits soon lifted, though, knowing the good doctor's patients included such notables of the time as Eddie Fisher, Tennessee Williams, and Elizabeth Taylor. Celebrities could afford the best medical care; surely the doctor was above reproach. Mantle, however, would have been better off taking any mother's advice: drink lots of liquids, get plenty of rest, take two aspirin, and tough it out.

"He greets me at the door wearing a white smock with bloodstains all over it," Mantle recalled in *The Mick*. "Like a lamb I followed him into his office." When the doctor jabbed

Mantle with a smoky liquid-filled syringe, he screamed. "It felt as though he had stuck a red-hot poker into me," Mantle remembered. "I'm paralyzed."

Mantle barely made it back to his hotel. The next morning he woke to find he could hardly move. Mantle ended up in Lenox Hill Hospital, where they lanced the wound, cutting a three-inch star over the hipbone and then letting it drain. "It left a hole so big you could put a golf ball in it," he recalled.

That was it for Mantle's run at Ruth's record. He had to settle for 54 homers and stand by while Maris took it all the way to the last game of the season.

At 154 games, Maris had 59 home runs. Going into the final game, on October 1, he was tied with the Babe. In his second at-bat, in the fourth inning, on a 2-0 pitch from Red Sox pitcher Tracy Stallard, Maris hit one 10 rows deep in the right-field stands. Maris had done it.

"No player ever accomplished so much and enjoyed it so little," Mantle said of his teammate's triumph, in *All My Octobers*. "Too nervous to enjoy the cheers when he heard them, and unable to ignore the boos that came when the cheering stopped."

Mantle had no regrets in losing the home-run derby. "I didn't lose," he said in *The Mick*. "I won over the fans, and out of it came a beautiful friendship between me and Roger."

A HERO AGAIN

Being the competitor he was, the determined defier of pain, Mantle literally struggled out of his hospital bed to play in the 1961 World Series. He and his team had the previous year's defeat to avenge.

Mantle missed the first two games in Yankee Stadium, in which the Yankees and the Cincinnati Reds split. He made it into the third game at Crosley Field, but went hitless in four at-bats. In the fourth game, Mantle took to the field with blood on his uniform. Earlier, the team doctor had dressed the wound

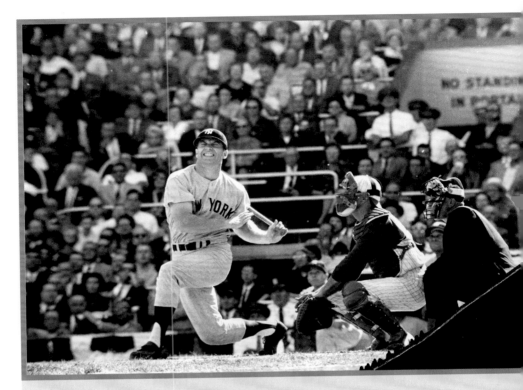

Grimacing in pain, Mickey Mantle swung at a pitch during the 1961 World Series against the Cincinnati Reds. An injection from an incompetent doctor left Mantle with a hip infection and ended his run against Roger Maris to beat Babe Ruth's home-run record. Mantle was able to appear in the World Series, though play aggravated his wound, which bled through his uniform.

with layers of gauze. Still, the blood came. "I drilled a line drive off the wall in center, normally a cinch double," Mantle remembered in *All My Octobers*. "This time I had to stop at first. I stood there gritting my teeth, breaking into a cold sweat, blood rolling down my leg and soaking through my uniform."

Mantle made no display of the wound suffered at the hands of an incompetent doctor. He did not seek sympathy. Still, teammate Johnny Blanchard got a glimpse of how bad the gouge was while in the clubhouse during Game 4. "[The surgical wound] was from the bone up, not from the skin down," he said, as reported in Castro's biography. "The way the wound was dressed was first with a coating of sulfur right down on the bone, by the hip where it was, then it was covered with gauze and then bandaged over. It was unbelievable this guy could walk, much less play."

Mantle was hemorrhaging. Yet play he did. Though his scoring contribution in the Yankees' four-games-to-one crushing of the Reds amounted to little, the fans were with Mantle every agonizing step of the way. "After Roger beat me in the home-run race in 1961," Mantle said, as quoted in *Mickey Mantle: America's Prodigal Son*, "I could do no wrong. Everywhere I went I got standing ovations. All I had to do was walk on the field."

In looking back at the season and the home-run derby, Mantle was insightful. "They wouldn't forgive Roger for not being Babe Ruth," he reflected in *All My Octobers*. "They finally forgave me for not being Joe DiMaggio. For the first time they saw me as an underdog, making it a race, playing hurt. In a way I had not heard before, they cheered me for what I did and what I might have done."

A Player's Player

For Mickey Mantle, baseball always came first. It was his life; it had always been his life. When he played, and he had an indomitable urge to play, there was no other world. Baseball was all Mantle knew.

A major-league ballplayer is away from home more than half the year. From April to September, there are the regular-season games—162 of them. With spring training, possible postseason competition (a regularity for a Yankee), and maybe a tour of the Far East or Latin America, the play-day calendar stretched even further. A man on an active roster could spend as much as two-thirds of the year chasing a baseball. It is estimated that, over the 18 years Mickey Mantle competed, he logged a cumulative 12 years on the job, hitting and fielding a five-ounce, rubber-coated sphere.

Everyone is all smiles in this Mantle family portrait from 1965. Mickey and Merlyn Mantle gathered with their children, *(from left)* David, Danny, Billy, and Mickey, Jr. Baseball kept Mantle away from his family for as much as two-thirds of the year. "I didn't spend the time with them that my dad had spent with me," Mantle wrote in *The Mick*.

The resulting absence from home could take an alarming toll on an athlete's family life. For Mantle, the price extracted was heavy, indeed. As Tony Castro observed in his biography, *Mickey Mantle: America's Prodigal Son,* "After 1961, he [Mantle] was the hero of New York but a virtual stranger to his family."

"It's taken a lot of years, but now I can finally admit to myself that I gave Merlyn everything she wanted except having me around enough," Mantle recalled in *The Mick*, published in 1985. "I was no better father than I was a husband. I've been to my kids just about like I've been to Merlyn. I didn't spend the time with them that my dad had spent with me."

For Mantle, drinking and downing the serious stuff helped ease the pain of being away from home. With long, often lonely nights on the road, he ritualistically retreated into the comfort of a bar, hard liquor his best friend.

There were times, more than a few, when alcohol, or, more precisely, its effects, accompanied Mantle right out onto the playing field. Early in 1963, in a series against Baltimore, Mantle had been put on the disabled list. Unconcerned with the need to compete the following day, the "Oklahoma Kid" got good and plastered the night before. During the next day's game, in the ninth inning, while stooped over in the dugout and barely able to stand, Mantle was called off the bench to play. Manager Ralph Houk had instantly reinstated him on the active list.

On the first pitch, a fastball around Mantle's eyes, he made direct contact, smashing the pellet over the center-field fence. "Hitting the ball was easy," he murmured, as reported in Castro's biography. "Running around the bases was the tough part."

MICKEY'S CALLED SHOT

Though Mantle received his third MVP award in 1962, the following year was not a good one for the "Switch-Hitting Slugger" or for his team. Mantle played but 65 games, plagued, as usual, by injuries. And though the Yankees won the pennant by 10½ games, they went on to lose the Series to the Dodgers. Losing the Fall Classic was rare, but, when it happened, bearable. What occurred this time, however, was devastating. Never, since the Bronx Bombers played their first Series in

1921, had they ever been swept. In 1963, the now Los Angeles Dodgers took them in four.

Earlier in the season, on June 5, Mantle sustained his most debilitating injury in years. In a game against Baltimore, Mantle suffered a broken bone in his left foot when he crashed into the center-field fence chasing a fly ball in the sixth inning. He would be out for two months.

"Thinking he could reach the ball," the *New York Times* reported, "Mantle jumped high while running toward the 8-foot wire barrier. As he came down, his left foot was caught in the mesh wiring and twisted so that he broke the third metatarsal bone." The *Times* went on to point out, "The Yanks, as usual in a battle for the league lead, can't afford the loss of such a valuable man for too long."

The Yankees faced a new, revitalized Dodger team in the Series, a team they had defeated in three of four postseason contests since Mantle had become a Yankee in 1951. This year, with the likes of Sandy Koufax, Don Drysdale, and Johnny Podres facing them on the mound, it was no contest. All anyone could talk about after the Series was Koufax. Yogi Berra, who would become the Yankees' manager the following year, said it all when he declared, as quoted in *All My Octobers*, "I can see how he won 25 games. What I don't understand is how he lost five."

Although Mantle had to endure a major operation on his left knee early in 1964, he managed to play in all but 19 games that year, the best he had done since 1961. Yet the Yankees, facing the Cardinals in the World Series, lost the Fall Classic for the second time in a row, four games to three. In the third game, Mantle hit a home run off Barney Schultz that became known as his "called shot." While heading to the plate, Mantle was to have said to teammate Elston Howard, as reported in *Mickey Mantle: America's Prodigal Son*, "Ellie, you might as well go on to the clubhouse and start getting dressed, 'cause I'm ending this game right now." Mickey's round-tripper won it, 2-1.

VICIOUS CYCLE

"A PUZZLER: WHERE TO PUT MANTLE?" read the headline on Leonard Koppett's March 24, 1965, article in the *New York Times*. "The shape of the problem is clear, and not new," the writer went on to explain. "Mantle's legs, injured and reinjured over 15 years, have reduced his mobility. He can't get around as a center fielder." Koppett did add, however, "At the same time, his [Mantle's] batting power and leadership qualities are undiminished."

In the previous week, the new Yankee manager, Johnny Keane, had placed Mantle in right field, hoping that with less territory to cover, the slugger would comport himself adequately. No good. "He has had as much trouble in starting, stopping, turning, changing direction, planting his feet for quick throws and cutting off balls to either side that his defensive handicaps would hurt the club in right field almost as much as in center," Koppett observed.

For Mantle, it was a familiar problem, one that formed a vicious cycle. "Among other things," Keane was quoted as saying, "this fellow has a lot of difficulty getting into the kind of shape that might prevent injury, because his legs won't let him do enough of the kind of work it takes to get into perfect shape." Clearly, for Mantle, it was a no-win situation.

In the end, Mantle played right, left, and center field throughout the season, being relatively ineffective at all three spots. "To make a long story short, I ended up real unhappy about the whole season," Mantle reflected in *The Mick*. "Playing 122 games, I only hit .255. The lowest point of my career by far."

The Yankees themselves were not doing much better than their celebrated hitter. The 1964 World Series would be Mantle's last, and the team's last until 1976. The Yanks wound up in sixth place in 1965, far away from any pennant. Players were hitting .193, .229, and .235—not the Yankee averages of old. "If I were a Yankee hater, I'd say it was about time," pitcher Jim Bouton was quoted as saying in the June 6 issue of the *New York Times*. "But I still wouldn't bet on it."

On September 18, Mantle played in his 2,000th game as a Yankee. The organization gave their star attraction a "Mickey Mantle Day at Yankee Stadium" in celebration. It would be the first of four such commemorations to come. A sellout crowd packed the Stadium. Large banners reading, "Don't Quit Mick," were strung everywhere. The fans had reason for concern. Maybe, after 15 seasons racing around chasing a baseball, with plenty of scars to prove it, it was time to say goodbye?

BACKYARD FOOTBALL

As the 1960s crossed their midpoint, and as the nation began its slow, painful recovery from the assassination of President Kennedy in November 1963, Mickey Mantle, too, took time to take stock. "The times," as singer/songwriter Bob Dylan would report, "they are a-changing." This was true for the world, the nation, and for an aging, injury-prone ballplayer named Mantle.

"At 34 years of age, the renowned switch-hitting star of the New York Yankees can neither run well nor throw well, and probably can bat only right-handed," Joseph Durso reported in the *New York Times*, referring to Mantle. "He suffers from weak knees, aching legs, a mysteriously sore right shoulder, and increasing moods of melancholy."

"Whenever it looked like the Yankees didn't want me, that would be the end of it," Durso went on to quote Mantle. "I could probably tell."

Not wanting Mantle was not an option for his ball club, however. Just having Mantle on the team was an inspiration to his teammates; he was a player's player. And he filled the seats, as fans wanted to see their idol in any capacity. Besides, at the end of the 1965 season, Mantle had hit "only" 473 home runs. "I'd like to get 500," the switch-hitting slugger told Durso.

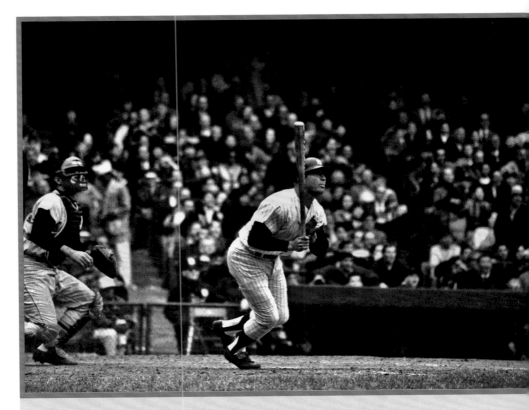

Mickey Mantle's many injuries really began to catch up with him in the mid-1960s, with his season batting averages dropping below .300. Still, on May 14, 1967, against the Orioles, Mantle slugged the 500th home run of his career. Here, he watches that homer as it sails into the right-field stands.

"I should have 500 by now." As play began in 1966, that left Mantle with but 27 homers to go.

There was a problem, though. In November of the previous year, Mantle tore up his shoulder playing backyard football with his son Mickey, Jr., and brothers Roy and Ray. "I was running out for a pass when one of the twins blindsided me," Mantle remembered in *The Mick*. "My shoulder was hurt.

I knew it was serious. I knew right away it was going to affect my career."

A visit to the famed Mayo Clinic confirmed the worst. Mantle had bone chips and calcium deposits in the shoulder. An operation took place immediately. His doctor told Mantle that the shoulder would be all right, to give it a little rest, and with luck he would be knocking them over the wall again. Mantle reported for spring training in February.

Mantle's numbers were up slightly in 1966; he hit 23 home runs and 56 RBIs, and batted .288. For the team, however, it was the worst season in memory. The Yankees finished last in the American League. Mantle was now playing for the worst team in baseball.

The "Oklahoma Kid" knew the end was near. In 1967, the Yankees switched him to first base, a move designed to take the strain off his knees. Playing first turned out to be harder, not easier, on Mantle's knees. He was adequate at best in his new fielding position.

But on May 14, in Yankee Stadium, batting left-handed against Baltimore Orioles pitcher Stu Miller, Mantle achieved a lifetime goal—he smashed his 500th home run. He would go on to make it 536 before retirement.

OUT

"I can't see the ball anymore," Mickey Mantle told George Vecsey, of the *New York Times*. "I can't steal second when I need to anymore. I can't go from first to third anymore, and I think it's time to quit trying."

On March 1, 1969, Mantle made it official; he was retiring from baseball. Marvin Miller, president of the Major League Baseball Players' Association, had called him "a gimpy 36-year-old first baseman with 66-year-old-legs," as reported by Tony Castro. Mantle himself realized there was no putting off retirement. His legs had become so sore, there were days in the 1968 season when he could hardly get out of the dugout. In

After 18 seasons with the New York Yankees, Mickey Mantle announced his retirement on March 1, 1969, during a news conference in Fort Lauderdale, Florida. At right was Ralph Houk, who again was the Yankees' manager.

any other occupation, with 15 fractures, injuries, or surgeries, Mantle would have been declared disabled.

In 1968, his last year as a Yankee, Mantle hit but .237. It killed him, killed him to go out with such a low number. Worse, his lifetime average had now dropped below .300, the symbolic benchmark in baseball. Mantle averaged .298 throughout his 18-year career. It made him want to cry.

"I played in more than 2,400 games, more than any Yankee player in history, and I hit 536 home runs, and I

☆ ☆ ☆ ☆ ☆ ☆

ONE SMALL STEP . . .

The year that Mickey Mantle retired from baseball and walked out of the ballpark, Neil Armstrong, commander of the Apollo 11 mission, landed his *Eagle* spacecraft on the Moon and walked out onto an alien world. In the public eye, both events ended a tumultuous decade.

"That's one small step for a man, one giant leap for mankind," Commander Armstrong announced, as he stepped out of his lunar module and touched the surface of the Moon. In doing so, on July 20, 1969, Armstrong, representing the Apollo program, indeed, the entire nation, fulfilled a national goal set by President John F. Kennedy early in his administration. In between, the country had gone through the momentous change and upheaval that was the 1960s.

There was the young president's assassination itself, in Dallas, Texas, on November 22, 1963. Anyone over 10 at the time remembers to this day exactly where he or she was and what they were doing the moment they heard the tragic news. Kennedy's death marked a loss of a national innocence from which the country has yet to recover.

Begun in earnest in the mid-1950s, the civil-rights movement took flight with numerous marches, sit-ins, and confrontations in the '60s. Led by the Reverend Martin

shouldn't be griping about my career," Mantle was quoted as saying in *Mickey Mantle: America's Prodigal Son.* "But I know it should have been so much better, and the big reason it wasn't is the lifestyle I chose, the late nights and too many empty glasses."

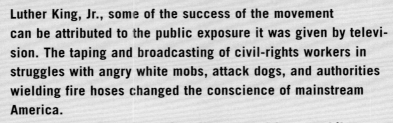

☆ ☆ ☆ ☆ ☆ ☆

Luther King, Jr., some of the success of the movement can be attributed to the public exposure it was given by television. The taping and broadcasting of civil-rights workers in struggles with angry white mobs, attack dogs, and authorities wielding fire hoses changed the conscience of mainstream America.

On August 2, 1964, United States naval forces, while on an intelligence mission in support of covert South Vietnamese attacks on North Vietnam, came under attack by North Vietnamese torpedo boats. Subsequently, President Lyndon B. Johnson was able to get Congress to pass the Gulf of Tonkin Resolution, which gave him, among other things, the power to conduct military operations without a declaration of war. The war did not end for another 11 years, after more than 58,000 Americans lost their lives.

The Moon landing seemed to restore, if only temporarily, America's confidence in itself and in its future. Landing two astronauts on the Moon, 240,000 miles (386,000 kilometers) from home and returning them safely to Earth was a momentous technical and logistic achievement. Twelve astronauts in all would make six trips to the Moon's surface from 1969 to 1972. It was a proud time to be an American.

In his last season at bat, Mantle was often given gift pitches and rousing cheers, a sign of the respect that other teams and adoring fans had for the legend. Mantle knew what was happening, of course. "It's all sentiment," he remarked, as quoted in *Mickey Mantle: Stories & Memorabilia from a Lifetime with the Mick.* "I'm not sure I like that. They sure as hell aren't cheering me for my batting average."

Still, while going out a hero was great, ending is always tough. "I don't know how I'll feel not playing ball," Mantle said to George Vecsey the day after he retired. "I've been playing ball for 20 years, and I'll probably miss it like crazy."

One person who would not be sorry to see Mickey's playing days end, however, was his wife, Merlyn. "I don't know how my four boys feel about it," Mickey said, "but my wife has been after me to quit for three years. I know she's happy."

Working
the Game

Mickey Mantle was going to miss baseball—most of it, anyway.

He certainly would long for his teammates. Whitey Ford, Billy Martin, and Hank Bauer were all gone, out of the game or off the team. Others, though, were still around, those with whom Mantle had connected and who had come to revere him, not just for the player he was, but for the kind of teammate they needed. Mel Stottlemyre recalled in *Our Mickey*:

> I remembered the first day I arrived at the Stadium, a frightened kid, just overwhelmed—22 years old, and here I was walking into the clubhouse at the famous Yankee Stadium. . . . I put on my uniform facing the wall, and nobody came near me. I think I was just straightening my hat and

getting ready to go on the field for the first time in a Yankee uniform. A guy came over and I heard him say hello and welcome to the club. I looked up and it was Mickey Mantle. I couldn't even tell you how big that was to me. We became very close friends.

Mantle would miss the fans, too, and his conflicted relationship with them. To be sure, the bond was not always positive. "There were all those times he would push little kids aside when they wanted his autograph," Jim Bouton, author of *Ball Four,* one of the best-selling sports books ever, said. "I've seen him slam a bus window on kids trying to get his autograph."

Mantle, though, came to appreciate the upside of fan-based fame: to be able to walk into a restaurant without reservations, to have his car parked for him. "Most fans are considerate and would like nothing better than to find an excuse to do you a personal kindness," he said in *Mickey Mantle: The Education of a Baseball Player.* "You can work out ways of dodging the pests, and the few irritations that do arise are a very small price to pay for the advantages that accrue."

Of course, there would also be the money; Mantle would miss his salary, one of the highest in baseball at the time he retired. It's no secret that the Yankee superstar played, hung on, the last two years primarily for the money, the $100,000 contracts.

When Mantle quit baseball on March 1, 1969, when he came to understand there would be no 1969 season, reality finally took hold. "Gradually, the realization hit me," he recalled in *The Mick.* "Baseball was over. The $100,000-a-year salary was gone. My bowling alley in Dallas had closed years before. I was thirty-seven years old with a family to support. I had to start making a new life. But what was I going to do?"

Mantle may have been out of the game, but he still had to earn a living—a living beyond baseball.

Former Yankees and new Hall of Famers Mickey Mantle *(left)* and Whitey Ford *(right)* received congratulations from their former manager Casey Stengel after induction ceremonies for the two men in 1974. Mantle was elected to the Hall of Fame in his first year of eligibility.

HALL OF FAME

One thing Mantle would not need to worry about was his place in the sport's pantheon. In 1974, the first year in which he was eligible, Mantle was inducted into the Baseball Hall of Fame. He received 322 out of 365 votes cast—88 percent. Former teammate Whitey Ford joined Mantle for the honor, though it would not be in his first year of eligibility.

In his Hall of Fame speech, Mantle, not the most comfortable speaker, began by apologizing for all the strikeouts he had racked up. "I broke Babe Ruth's record for all-time strikeouts," he declared. "He only had, like, 1,500, I think. I ended up with 1,710. So that's one that no one will ever break probably, because, if you strike out that much, you don't get to play very long. I just lucked out."

Mantle went on to credit his dad with just about everything he had achieved since becoming a big leaguer. "He had the foresight to realize that someday in baseball that left-handed hitters were going to hit against right-handed pitchers and right-handed hitters were going to hit against left-handed pitchers; and he taught me, he and his father, to switch-hit at a real young age," Mantle explained. What his father insisted on worked for the young Mickey. In the first year he came up, Casey Stengel began to platoon everyone, to Mantle's advantage.

Mantle continued by acknowledging his mother's hard work, and in so doing, reminded his audience of his impoverished roots. "We didn't have a lot of money or anything," he said. "She used to make my uniforms, and we would buy the cleats or get 'em off of somebody else's shoes or somethin' and then we would take 'em and have 'em put into a pair of my street shoes that were getting old."

The speech was pure Mickey, unadulterated "country bumpkin." From a humble background, Mantle had risen to the top of his game. A Triple Crown year, three Most Valuable Player awards, 18 World Series home runs, and now the Hall of

Fame; in baseball there was nothing more for the "Oklahoma Kid" to achieve.

SUCH A DEAL!

But the now ex-Yankee still had to earn a living.

Early on, in his first season as a New York slugger, naive country boy Mickey Mantle had been suckered into a promotional deal that the Yankee management had to bail him out of. Mantle remained vulnerable to such business promotions all his life.

There was a bowling alley in Dallas, in a crummy, tacky shopping center that finally went under.

His "Mantle Men and Namath Women Employment Agency," in partnership with football legend Joe Namath, never took off.

Mickey Mantle's Country Cookin' restaurant chain sought to capitalize on the growing fast-food phenomenon of the 1970s. "We went public in June 1969," Mantle recalled in *The Mick*. "I was chairman of the board. I had 110,000 shares of stock. At an offering price of $15 a share, I immediately became a millionaire—on paper." Mantle was lucky to get out of the business without a brush with the Securities and Exchange Commission.

There was even the Canadian Bomb Shelter Survival Corporation, which was to have built bomb shelters throughout Canada and then expand into the United States. It bombed!

There were successes, too, especially those built on Mantle's personal appearances and the growing memorabilia demand for his signature and his baseball cards. Mantle was learning to work the game.

In a bizarre incident, reported by business partner Bill Liederman in *Our Mickey*, Mantle was asked to make an appearance at a 13-year-old's bar mitzvah. The young man's father wanted to hire Mantle to show up so he could show

As the sports memorabilia craze took off in the 1980s, Mickey Mantle's autograph became worth plenty of money. As he traveled to memorabilia conventions and card shows, Mantle also gained new popularity. Here, he signs baseballs in his home in 1990.

him off. Mantle, who probably did not even know what a bar mitzvah was, tried to get rid of the man by demanding a $50,000 price tag. "Deal!" the father said, to the astonishment of everyone. Mantle made the appearance and was reported to have had a great time.

And, of course, there was the opening of Mickey Mantle's Restaurant & Sports Bar in New York City at 42 Central Park South in 1988. It became one of New York's most popular restaurants, with Mantle's original Yankee Stadium Monument Park plaque displayed at the front entrance.

With one enterprise after another, as the 1980s rolled on, Mantle obtained a level of financial security befitting his fame and stature. Basically, he created a second "career," that of signing his name. It would soon become more profitable than his final years with the Yankees.

Still, the drinking continued, the slide into personal dysfunction more and more apparent. Radio show host Don Imus famously joked on the air, as reported on Wikipedia, "If you get to Mickey Mantle's restaurant after midnight, you win a free dinner if you can guess which table Mickey's under."

BANNED FROM BASEBALL

In 1983, Mickey Mantle signed a lucrative, $100,000-a-year deal as a "corporate greeter." The problem was with the place he chose to represent. It was the Claridge Hotel and Casino in Atlantic City—a high-class gambling joint. As Mantle should have known, baseball commissioner Bowie Kuhn was not going to take kindly to the association of baseball and gambling, no matter how tenuous.

Willie Mays had done something similar in signing with Bally's Park Place, across the street from Claridge's. In response, Kuhn banned Mays from baseball for life.

Mantle was threatened with the same action should he take the Claridge job. Mantle did not see it as much of a warning. "Some threat," he said in *The Mick*. "What would I be banned from? Since my retirement, I had been a Yankee batting instructor during spring training. What it really amounted to was a two-week paid vacation for me and Merlyn."

Mantle took the job. Mantle was banned from baseball.

Mantle figured he never lost a dime on the deal because he was not doing anything official for baseball. Still, he thought the whole thing stunk. He had been going to golf tournaments for years sponsored by the Riviera Hotel, a casino in

★ ★ ★ ★ ☆

MEMORABILIA MADNESS

Believe it or not, the first baseball cards, printed in the 1880s, were placed in cigarette packs. This was done partially to promote the cigarettes but also to protect the fragile smokes from damage. One of the most famous cards, issued in 1909, featured Hall of Famer Honus Wagner, a guy who never took a drag. In 2007, a T-206 Wagner card, considered the "Mona Lisa" of baseball cards, was sold for $2,350,000.

The modern era of baseball cards began in 1948, with the issuing of black-and-white editions by the Bowman Gum Company. Naturally, the cards came with a stick of gum.

In 1951, the Topps Chewing Gum Company published its first cards. The company has dominated the market to this day. In 1952, Topps was farsighted enough to put out a Mickey Mantle card, #311. In the early 1980s, Mantle was to have said, "I don't know why my rookie card was worth $12,000 and somebody else's is $200 or $300." Recently, a Topps Mickey Mantle #311 card sold for $50,000.

In the 1970s, as baby boomers, those born from 1946 to 1964, began looking to recapture their youth, they sought to purchase the baseball cards that were links to their past.

Las Vegas. Joe DiMaggio was co-chairman of the tournament. To Mantle, it was a double standard he could not abide.

For nearly two years, Mantle stayed away from baseball. Then, with the ascendance of Peter Ueberroth to the commissioner's office in October 1984, a re-evaluation took place. "Mr. Ueberroth himself called me on the afternoon of Sunday, March 17, 1985, to invite me to New York for an announcement," Mantle recalled in *The Mick.* "And on March 18, Willie

☆ ☆ ☆ ☆ ☆ ☆

Demand soared for such cards, and, along with it, prices. Cards that originally sold for pennies were now worth dollars. Soon, they went into the hundreds, then into the thousands of dollars. At some of today's card shows, real money trades hands.

Mickey Mantle never made much from baseball cards, not his collection, anyway. He gave most away, including the ones of himself. It soon became apparent, however, that Mantle's autograph, scribbled on anything remotely connected with baseball, was worth plenty. Items like photographs, balls, bats, even clothing, became instant collectibles once it was possible to verify the authenticity of Mantle's signature on them. In the 1980s, as Mantle found himself traveling to card shows and memorabilia conventions around the country, his popularity only grew. At times, Mantle was paid as much as $50,000 per weekend just to sign his name.

In 1989, Mickey Mantle closed a memorabilia deal with Upper Deck, an up-and-coming card company, that would bring him millions. There was money to be made on baseball, after baseball, and Mantle did not hesitate to cash in.

Willie Mays, Mickey Mantle, and baseball commissioner Peter Ueberroth *(center)* posed for a picture in Major League Baseball's offices in New York in March 1985. The previous commissioner, Bowie Kuhn, had banned Mays and Mantle from baseball after they had taken jobs representing casino-hotels. Ueberroth reinstated both men.

Mays and I appeared at the Astor Salon of the Waldorf Astoria with the commissioner and were officially welcomed back to baseball."

The ban had infuriated fans, of course. They were only too happy to cheer their national icons' return.

TIME FOR THE PAIN

In 1988, Mickey separated from his wife, Merlyn. Though they would not divorce, they never lived together again.

Mantle blamed himself for the estrangement. He expressed tremendous guilt over the way he had treated his wife and the children. Yes, he had been an absent husband at best, an unfaithful one at worst. In the end, both husband and wife attributed the fundamental cause of the marriage's failure to alcohol. In the latter years of their marriage, Merlyn, too, had taken to the bottle. Oftentimes, as long as Mantle took her along for the ride, she found little cause to complain about her husband's behavior. "I decided that, if he needed someone who parked her butt on a barstool and drank with him all night, I could be that person," she said in *A Hero All His Life.* "I started to travel with him more, but I knew I couldn't be a guard dog the rest of my life."

Merlyn was not Mickey's only drinking buddy, however. Frequently he took his sons with him to the saloons. All four developed drinking problems.

Mantle now also suffered from anxiety, or what is today referred to as a panic attack. On a flight home to Dallas, Mantle began to hyperventilate. He thought he was having a heart attack. Fortunately that was not the case. Alcohol was the problem.

Throughout it all, the pain, the physical pain, never stopped. Degenerative arthritis had set into his legs, not a surprising development for a man his age having gone through the abuse he had.

Mentally, Mantle was also in torment. He often plunged into depression. Though he had escaped death by 40, something that surprised him as much as it relieved him, Mantle knew he was mortal. He would laugh at a joke going around that talked of his arrival at Heaven's gate after he died. In the gag, St. Peter says, "Mick, we can't let you in on account of the kind of life you've lived down on Earth. But before you go to that other place, God wanted to know if you'd sign these two dozen balls for him."

10

"Yesterday When I Was Young"

It's hard to know whether it was the public displays of drunken misbehavior or the recurring memory losses that finally drove Mickey Mantle to seek professional help. Maybe it was both.

In late September 1993, Mantle was invited to participate in a charity golf tournament for the Harbor Club Children's Christmas Fund near Atlanta, Georgia. Having downed Bloody Marys all day, Mantle was tipsy when he arrived for dinner. During the ceremony, Mantle referred, out loud, to the organizer of the event, the Reverend Wayne Monroe, using words unfit to print. When Mantle sobered up the next day, he was mortified to discover what had happened. There were those, however, who chose to remind Mantle that it was not the first time he had acted so despicably.

Then there were the memory losses, the blackouts. They had been occurring for six years now. "The loss of memory really scared me," Mantle said, as reported in *Mickey Mantle: America's Prodigal Son.* "I told a couple of the doctors I played golf with that I thought I had Alzheimer's disease, and they said, 'Well you're probably not there yet.'. . . I was scared it was alcohol that changed my brain."

It was. Blackouts are a sign that alcohol is short-circuiting the brain's wiring.

In December 1993, Mantle sat for a complete physical. Blood work showed that the Yankee superstar had a diseased liver. Magnetic resonance imaging (MRI) confirmed the diagnosis. The next day, Mantle's doctor laid it on the line. "Look, I'm not going to lie to you," he said, as quoted in Castro's biography. "The next drink might be your last."

Pat Summerall, a longtime friend, sportscaster, and, just as important, a recovering alcoholic, was the one to intervene, to prod Mantle to get the help he so desperately needed. On January 7, 1994, Mantle entered the famed Betty Ford Center in Rancho Mirage, California—the rehab clinic to the stars. He would remain there for more than a month, 33 days. The previous September, Mickey's son Danny had checked himself into the Betty Ford Center. He would be joined later by his wife, Kay. Rehab was becoming a Mantle family affair.

"If I knew I was going to make it to 50, I would have taken better care of myself," Mantle had been saying over and over in recent years, as reported in numerous biographies. The 62-year-old former outfielder could not go back and redo his 43-year battle with alcohol, of course. But as George Vecsey, writing in the *New York Times* on January 30, 1994, put it, "The decision to seek help means the Mick might make it to 65 or 70."

"I'M MICK AND I'M AN ALCOHOLIC"

The Betty Ford Center is a no-nonsense drug- and alcohol-abuse-recovery facility. Though it is famous for taking in the famous, once a person enters the sprawling desert complex, all pretense is quickly drained from the patient. According to Vecsey of the *New York Times,* "The counselors try to break through the chemical haze and the arrogance and the denial, to persuade the performers and the political figures and the athletes that they really do have a lot in common with the skid-row drunk or the street junkie."

For Mantle, it was confession time. It was not easy. Mantle thought he would pass out from nervousness and embarrassment when he got up to declare, "I'm Mick and I'm an alcoholic." In an interview months later, Mantle said, as reported in *Mickey Mantle: America's Prodigal Son,* "One thing I really screwed up, besides baseball, was being a father. . . . My kids have never blamed me for not being there. They don't have to. I blame myself."

One of the hardest things Mantle had to do at the Betty Ford Center was to write his father a letter and tell him how he felt about the man who died at 39. "You talk about sad," Mantle began, as quoted in Castro's biography. "It took me 10 minutes to write the letter, and I cried the whole time. . . . I told him I had four boys—he died before my first son, Mickey, Jr., was born—and I told him that I loved him. I wish I could have told him that when he was still alive."

Mantle left the Betty Ford Center sober, determined to rededicate himself to his family, fans, and his place in the game of baseball. On March 12, he confronted his first major test of strength when he was told his son Billy, age 36, had died of Hodgkin's disease. Telling Merlyn was the most agonizing thing he ever had to do.

Billy, Mickey's second-youngest son, had been at his own alcohol-rehabilitation facility as part of his third conviction for driving while intoxicated. Though Billy died of the disease that killed his grandfather and great-grandfather, his drinking was a complicating factor in his death. Hodgkin's and alcohol—the family curses.

READY TO LEAD

Mickey Mantle emerged from rehab looking trimmer and sharper than he had in years. Friends said that he seemed younger by at least a decade. He swore to them that he would remain sober—and he did.

On July 9, Mantle returned in triumph to Yankee Stadium for Old-Timers' Day. Former teammates Whitey Ford and Clete Boyer gave him a good ribbing. "They were asking me, 'Did you know how to get in here sober?'" Mantle told Dave Anderson, of the *New York Times*. "But I'm sober today and I'll be sober tomorrow. . . . Whenever you get to where I was, it's a matter of life and death."

For now, anyway, it was all life.

In the spring, Mantle took to the airwaves, discussing on national television as openly and candidly as possible his career and addiction. With tears streaming down his cheeks, he told Bob Costas about his life. It was a monumental, emotional confession, one that only served to strengthen his loyalty with fans and, indeed, garner new ones. He taped television commercials urging kids not to drink, not to see him as a role model. "Talk about a role model," he said, as reported in *Mickey Mantle: Stories & Memorabilia from a Lifetime with the Mick*, "This is a role model. Don't be like me."

Mantle formed a foundation in honor of his son Billy. He said he felt more important as Mickey Mantle now than he had as a Yankee. Mantle was on a mission, undertaken to make amends. He promised Joe DiMaggio, currently a broadcaster, that he would help him with the Baseball Assistance Team (BAT), an organization to help old ballplayers with their problems. Mantle, an alcoholic for 43 years, looked forward to becoming a spokesman for the clean and sober life.

ONE DAY TO LIVE

Time, though, was not on Mickey Mantle's side. He had turned the page too late. On May 28, 1995, Mantle was hospitalized in Dallas, Texas, for a stomach ailment. "I guess it was just one of those things, like a virus," said Roy True, his business manager, as reported in the *New York Times*. "A little stomach disorder." Unfortunately, it was not. Mantle had liver cancer. He would need a liver transplant because the tumor could not be removed surgically.

Patients in Mantle's condition could usually expect a new liver in a month. On June 1, there were 4,659 patients waiting for livers throughout the United States, about 140 with liver cancer. Mantle received his transplanted liver on June 8, within 24 hours of being placed on the transplant waiting list. A liver donor was suddenly found overnight. The operation was a success, but during surgery doctors discovered that the cancer had spread.

Was Mickey Mantle given preferential treatment because he was a sports hero, a national celebrity? In the months to come, the debate on the issue raged. Who should get a liver? Should a 63-year-old alcoholic who brought his problems on himself go to the front of the line, ahead of younger, more temperate, patients? Should alcoholics with liver failure, obese people with heart disease, and smokers with lung cancer receive the same treatment as people who have lived lives of moderation? It was a question many asked, but few could really answer.

"People think I got that liver because of who I am," Mantle said later in an interview, as reported in *Mickey Mantle: America's Prodigal Son*. "but they have rules they go by. They told me I had one day to live. If I hadn't got this one, I wouldn't have made it."

Mantle, who would become a champion for donor transplants in the short time he had remaining, never lost his humor as his cancer spread. In joking with collector Barry Halper he asked if Halper wanted to buy his liver. Halper asked for the scalpel used to operate on Mantle instead.

(*continues on page 109*)

☆ ☆ ☆ ☆ ☆ ☆

ORGAN DONATIONS

Mickey Mantle was overwhelmed with the selfless gift of a liver from a stranger. In response, he directed that the Mickey Mantle Foundation be established to promote organ and tissue donations. Before he died, Mantle penned a personal message to his fans:

> The best gift I ever got was on June 8, 1995, when an organ donor gave me and five other patients at Baylor University Medical Center in Dallas the organs we needed to live. I guess you could say I got another time at bat.
>
> Now I want to give something back. I can do that first by telling kids and parents to take care of their bodies. Don't drink or do drugs. Your health is the main thing you've got, so don't blow it.
>
> Second, think hard about being an organ and tissue donor if the time ever comes. . . . Thanks for your prayers and kindness. I'll never be able to make up all I owe God and the American people. But if you will join me in supporting the cause of organ and tissue donation, it would be a great start.

The initial mission of the foundation is to eliminate the loss of life or the loss of quality of life because of the lack of organs and tissue available for transplantation. According to the foundation's Web site, "We must capture the minds and hearts of our fellow Americans. We must make it easier for families and loved ones to make this important decision during times of good health and clear thinking. We believe the American people will say 'Yes!' to organ and tissue donations."

Organ donation is the removal of specific tissues from a person who has recently died or from a living donor to transplant or

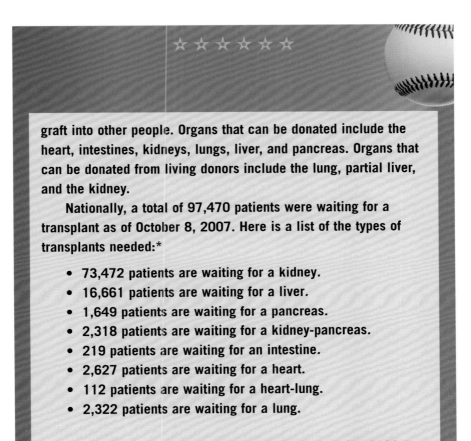

graft into other people. Organs that can be donated include the heart, intestines, kidneys, lungs, liver, and pancreas. Organs that can be donated from living donors include the lung, partial liver, and the kidney.

Nationally, a total of 97,470 patients were waiting for a transplant as of October 8, 2007. Here is a list of the types of transplants needed:*

- 73,472 patients are waiting for a kidney.
- 16,661 patients are waiting for a liver.
- 1,649 patients are waiting for a pancreas.
- 2,318 patients are waiting for a kidney-pancreas.
- 219 patients are waiting for an intestine.
- 2,627 patients are waiting for a heart.
- 112 patients are waiting for a heart-lung.
- 2,322 patients are waiting for a lung.

Here is the number of transplants performed during 2006:*

- 17,090 kidney transplants
- 6,650 liver transplants
- 463 pancreas transplants
- 924 kidney-pancreas transplants
- 175 intestine transplants
- 2,192 heart transplants
- 31 heart-lung transplants
- 1,405 lung transplants

* Statistics based on data from the Organ Procurement and Transplantation Network of the U.S. Department of Health and Human Services, as of October 8, 2007.

Mickey Mantle spoke to the media during a news conference on July 11, 1995, at the Baylor University Medical Center in Dallas, Texas. He had had a liver transplant on June 8, but the surgeons found that his cancer had spread. Chemotherapy left Mantle weakened.

(*continued from page 105*)
     Mickey left Baylor University Medical Center 20 days after entering. He would be required to return to the hospital for checkups, twice a week initially. Mantle would need to take drugs, in particular, chemotherapy, for at least the next three to six months, should he live that long.

     The hospital confinement and the surgery caused Mantle's muscles to atrophy. He did not look much like the Mickey Mantle of old. He looked skeletal. Yet Mantle was determined to soldier on. Earlier he had said, "I owe so much to God and to the American people," as reported in Castro's biography. "I'm going to spend the rest of my life trying to make it up."

"YESTERDAY WHEN I WAS YOUNG"

Mantle had little time left to do that, however. The chemotherapy treatments, which included cis-platinum, a nine-hour procedure resulting in nausea, vomiting, and weakness, were beginning to take their toll. On July 28, Mantle was readmitted to the hospital. Cancer had now spread to his right lung. "About two weeks ago, the doctors found a couple of spots of cancer in my lungs," Mantle said in a taped statement, reported in the August 2 edition of the *New York Times*. "Now I'm taking chemotherapy to get rid of the new cancer." Mantle the optimist.

     Yet what Mantle had was the most aggressive cancer anyone on his medical team had seen. In his final hours, it was left to Mantle's son David to take him off life support. On Sunday, August 13, 1995, at 1:10 A.M., at the age of 63, Mickey Mantle died.

     The pallbearers at Mantle's funeral were all former Yankee teammates: Whitey Ford, Bill Skowron, John Blanchard, Hank Bauer, Yogi Berra, and Bobby Murcer. Mantle had requested that entertainer Roy Clark sing his signature song, "Yesterday When I Was Young," at his funeral, the last lines of which read:

Some of Mickey Mantle's former teammates led the procession as Mantle's casket was carried from the church after his funeral service on August 15, 1995, in Dallas. Mantle had died two days earlier at the age of 63. The ex-teammates were *(in pairs from front)* Whitey Ford *(left)* and Yogi Berra; Bill Skowron and Hank Bauer; and John Blanchard and Bobby Murcer.

There are so many songs in me that won't be sung

I feel the bitter taste of tears upon my tongue

The time has come for me to pay for yesterday when I was young

Mantle felt the song pretty much summed up his life. Maybe?

"To remember Mickey Mantle as someone who drank himself to death, as an absentee husband and father who rained on his own parade, would be a disservice to the truth," writer Mickey Herskowitz said in *Mickey Mantle: Stories & Memorabilia from a Lifetime with the Mick.* "Mantle led a rich life, with an abundance of friends and merriment, more than he thought he deserved."

Bob Costas, a lifelong fan of Mickey Mantle, gave the eulogy at his fallen hero's funeral. "The facts of his life did not render untrue what was magnificent about him," Costas said, as recorded on the official Mickey Mantle Web site. "If anything, they made it more poignant."

Mantle, above all, wanted to be remembered as a good teammate. In that, and countless other respects, Herskowitz was quick to point out, Mantle was an overachiever.

In his eulogy, Costas summed up the "Oklahoma Kid" in a poignant and lasting sentence. "In the last year, Mickey Mantle, always so hard on himself, finally came to accept and appreciate that distinction between a role model and a hero. The first he often was not, the second he always will be."

Mickey Mantle, a fragile hero to be sure, but a hero nonetheless. A man whose humanity and humility always shined through.

STATISTICS

MICKEY MANTLE

Primary position: Center field (Also LF, RF, 1B)

Full name: Mickey Charles Mantle
Born: October 20, 1931, Spavinaw,
Oklahoma • Died: August 13, 1995,
Dallas, Texas • Height: 5'11" •
Weight: 198 lbs. • Teams: New York
Yankees (1951–1968)

YEAR	TEAM	G	AB	H	HR	RBI	BA
1951	NYY	96	341	91	13	65	.267
1952	NYY	142	549	171	23	87	.311
1953	NYY	127	461	136	21	92	.295
1954	NYY	146	543	163	27	102	.300
1955	NYY	147	517	158	37	99	.306
1956	NYY	150	533	188	52	130	.353
1957	NYY	144	474	173	34	94	.365
1958	NYY	150	519	158	42	97	.304
1959	NYY	144	541	154	31	75	.285
1960	NYY	153	527	145	40	94	.275
1961	NYY	153	514	163	54	128	.317
1962	NYY	123	377	121	30	89	.321
1963	NYY	65	172	54	15	35	.314
1964	NYY	143	465	141	35	111	.303

KEY: NYY = New York Yankees; G = Games; AB = At-bats; H = Hits; HR = Home runs;
RBI = Runs batted in; BA = Batting average

YEAR	TEAM	G	AB	H	HR	RBI	BA
1965	NYY	122	361	92	19	46	.255
1966	NYY	108	333	96	23	56	.288
1967	NYY	144	440	108	22	55	.245
1968	NYY	144	435	103	18	54	.237
TOTAL		2,401	8,102	2,415	536	1,509	.298

KEY: NYY = New York Yankees; G = Games; AB = At-bats; H = Hits; HR = Home runs; RBI = Runs batted in; BA = Batting average

CHRONOLOGY

1931   **October 20** Born in Spavinaw, Oklahoma.

1943   Plays second base in the Gabby Street League.

1946   Develops osteomyelitis after injury as a running back for Commerce High.

1947   Plays for the Baxter Springs Whiz Kids, a highly competitive semipro team.

1949   Signs contract with the Yankee organization; plays for the Class D Independence Yankees of the K-O-M League.

1950   Plays for the Class C Joplin Miners of the Western Association.

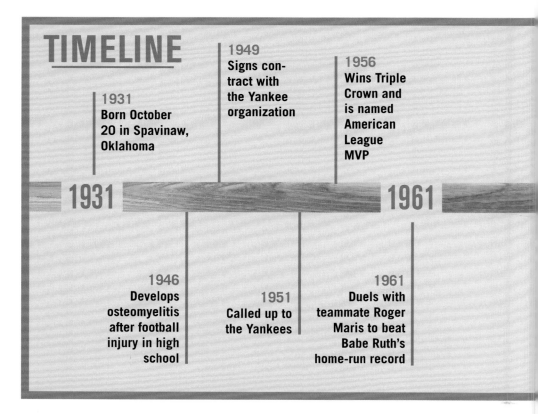

TIMELINE

1949
Signs contract with the Yankee organization

1931
Born October 20 in Spavinaw, Oklahoma

1956
Wins Triple Crown and is named American League MVP

1931 — **1961**

1946
Develops osteomyelitis after football injury in high school

1951
Called up to the Yankees

1961
Duels with teammate Roger Maris to beat Babe Ruth's home-run record

1951   Called up to the Yankees.

March 26 Hits 650-foot (198-meter) home run at Bovard Field on the University of Southern California campus.

October 5 Injures right knee in Game 2 of the World Series.

December 23 Marries Merlyn Johnson.

1952   **May 6** Elvin Mantle, Mickey's father, dies.

1953   **April 17** Hits a home run at Griffith Stadium in Washington that sails an estimated 565 feet.

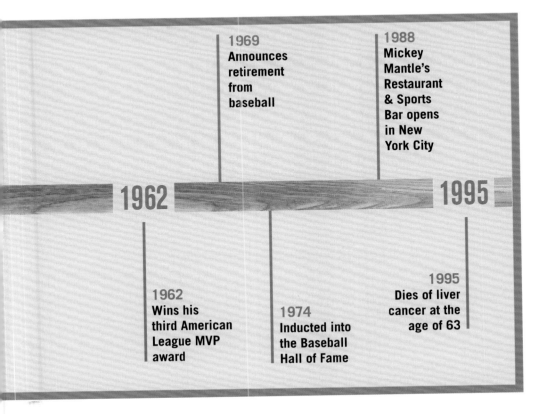

1969
Announces retirement from baseball

1988
Mickey Mantle's Restaurant & Sports Bar opens in New York City

1962

1995

1962
Wins his third American League MVP award

1974
Inducted into the Baseball Hall of Fame

1995
Dies of liver cancer at the age of 63

1956	Wins Triple Crown, leading the American League in batting average, home runs, and RBIs; is also named the American League Most Valuable Player.
1957	Repeats as American League Most Valuable Player.
1961	Duels with teammate Roger Maris in a race to break Babe Ruth's single-season home-run record of 60; Mantle is admitted to the hospital on September 9 for a hip infection and finishes the season with 54 home runs; Maris breaks the record with 61.
1962	Wins his third American League Most Valuable Player award.
1963	June 5 Breaks bone in left foot after crashing into the center-field fence chasing a fly ball.
1965	September 18 Mickey Mantle Day is held at Yankee Stadium to celebrate his 2,000th game as a Yankee.
1967	Begins to play first base for the Yankees.
1968	September 20 Hits home run No. 536, his last in the major leagues.
1969	March 1 Announces retirement from baseball.
1974	Inducted into the Baseball Hall of Fame.
1983	Banned from baseball for taking a job with a casino.
1985	Reinstated into baseball by new baseball commissioner Peter Ueberroth.
1988	Mickey Mantle's Restaurant & Sports Bar opens in New York City.
1994	January 7 Enters Betty Ford Center for treatment of alcoholism.
1995	May 28 Admitted to a hospital in Dallas for stomach pain.
	June 8 Undergoes liver transplant.
	August 13 Dies of liver cancer at the age of 63.

GLOSSARY

alcoholism   A chronic disorder marked by excessive and compulsive drinking of alcohol leading to psychological and physical dependence or addiction.

at-bat   An official turn at batting that is charged to a baseball player, except when the player walks, sacrifices, is hit by a pitched ball, or is interfered with by a catcher. At-bats are used to calculate a player's batting average and slugging percentage.

base on balls   The awarding of first base to a batter after a pitcher throws four balls. Also known as a walk, it is "intentional" when the four balls are thrown on purpose to avoid pitching to a batter.

baseball commissioner   The highest-ranking office in Major League Baseball.

batting average   The number of hits a batter gets divided by the number of times the player is at bat. For example, 3 hits in 10 at-bats would be a .300 batting average.

bunt   A ball hit softly so that it rolls to a particular spot in the infield. A bunt is usually hit by holding the bat loosely and letting the ball bounce off it rather than swinging the bat.

chemotherapy   The use of chemical agents in the treatment or control of disease—as in cancer.

cleanup hitter   The fourth batter in the lineup, usually a power hitter. The team hopes runners are on base for the "cleanup" hitter to drive home.

Dead Ball Era   A period in baseball from roughly 1900 to 1920 in which games were not high-scoring and the focus was more on fielding strategy than hitting home runs. The main batting strategy was to score runs through walks, base hits, bunts, and stolen bases.

diathermy   The generation of heat in tissue by electric currents for medical or surgical purposes.

drag bunt   When a left-handed batter lays down a bunt toward the right side of the infield that is out of reach of the pitcher. The batter may even stride toward first base as he bunts, appearing to drag the ball with him as he runs.

fastball   A ball thrown at a high velocity by the pitcher. Many of today's major-league pitchers can throw more than 90 miles per hour (145 kilometers per hour).

grand slam   A home run that is hit when the bases are loaded.

home run   When a batter hits a ball into the stands in fair territory, it is a home run. The batter may also have an inside-the-park home run if the ball never leaves the playing field and the runner is able to reach home plate without stopping before being tagged by a defensive player. A home run counts as one run, and if there are any runners on base when a home run is hit, they too score.

lineup   A list that is presented to the umpire and opposing coach before the start of the game that contains the order in which the batters will bat as well as the defensive fielding positions they will play.

Live Ball Era   The period in baseball after 1920 in which scores of games were significantly higher as teams began to focus their strategy on offense with powerful batters.

perfect game   A no-hitter in which each batter is retired consecutively, allowing no base runners through walks, errors, or any other means.

platoon   The practice of assigning two players to the same defensive position during a season, normally to complement a batter who hits well against left-handed pitchers with one who hits well against right-handed pitchers.

runs batted in   A statistic that reflects the number of runs a batter has scored with a hit or a walk. Also known as an RBI or ribbie.

shutout   A game in which a pitcher does not allow the opposing team to score a run. If the pitcher does not allow a hit, then the game is recorded as a no-hitter.

switch-hit   To hit from both sides of the plate—right-handed and left-handed.

Triple Crown   Won by the batter who leads the league at the end of the season in batting average, home runs, and runs batted in.

BIBLIOGRAPHY

BOOKS

Angell, Roger. *Game Time: A Baseball Companion.* New York: A Harvest Book/Harcourt Inc., 2003.

Bouton, Jim. *Ball Four.* New York: Wiley Publishing Inc., 1970.

Castro, Tony. *Mickey Mantle: America's Prodigal Son.* Dulles, Virginia: Brassey's Inc., 2002.

DiMaggio, Joe. *Lucky to Be a Yankee.* New York: Grosset & Dunlap, 1951.

Gillette, Gary, and Peter Palmer. *The 2006 ESPN Baseball Encyclopedia.* New York: Sterling Publishing Company Inc., 2006.

Halberstam, David. *Summer of '49.* New York: Harper Perennial Modern Classics, 1989.

Hall, John G. *Mickey Mantle: Before the Glory.* Leawood, Kansas: Leathers Publishing, 2005.

Herskowitz, Mickey, with Danny Mantle and David Mantle. *Mickey Mantle: Stories & Memorabilia from a Lifetime with the Mick.* New York: Stewart, Tabori & Chang, 2006.

Kennedy, Kevin, with Bill Gutman. *Twice Around the Bases: The Thinking Fan's Inside Look at Baseball.* New York: Harper, 2005.

Liederman, Bill, and Maury Allen. *Our Mickey: Cherished Memories of an American Icon.* Chicago: Triumph Books, 2003.

Mantle, Merlyn, Mickey Mantle, Jr., David Mantle, and Dan Mantle. *A Hero All His Life: A Memoir by the Mantle Family.* New York: HarperCollins, 1996.

Mantle, Mickey. *Mickey Mantle: The Education of a Baseball Player.* New York: Simon and Schuster, 1967.

————. *The Mick.* Garden City, N.Y.: Doubleday & Company, 1985.

Mantle, Mickey, and Mickey Herskowitz. *All My Octobers: My Memories of Twelve World Series When the Yankees Ruled Baseball.* New York: HarperCollins, 1994.

Mantle, Mickey, and Phil Pepe. *My Favorite Summer 1956.* New York: Doubleday, 1991.

Mnookin, Seth. *Feeding the Monster: How Money, Smarts, and Nerve Took a Team to the Top.* New York: Simon & Schuster, 2006.

Rampersad, Arnold. *Jackie Robinson: A Biography.* New York: Random House, 1997.

Vecsey, George. *Baseball: A History of America's Favorite Game.* New York: Random House, 2006.

Verducci, Tom. *The Baseball Book.* New York: Sports Illustrated Books, 2006

Williams, Ted, and John Underwood. *The Science of Hitting.* New York: Simon & Schuster, 1986.

NEWSPAPERS

Daley, Arthur. "Mantle's Home Town Plans All-Day Fete." *New York Times,* October 16, 1952.

————. "Sports of the Times." *New York Times,* March 21, 1952.

————. "Sports of the Times." *New York Times,* April 22, 1956.

Dawson, James. "Mantle, Yankees, in Outfield Shift." *New York Times,* February 24, 1951.

————. "New Lead-Off Man Stengel Problem." *New York Times,* October 6, 1951.

Durso, Joseph. "Mantle Is Beset by Doubt." *New York Times,* January 16, 1966.

Effrat, Louis. "Towering Drive by Yank Slugger Features 7-3 Defeat of Senators." *New York Times,* April 17, 1953.

————. "What a Change Mantle Hath Wrought in Fans." *New York Times,* June 22, 1956.

Koppett, Leonard. "A Puzzler: Where to Put Mantle?" *New York Times,* March 24, 1965.

Myerson, Allen. "Cancer From Mantle's Liver Spreads to Right Lung." *New York Times,* August 2, 1995.

Talese, Gay. "Mantle—the King Whose Homage Is Catcalls." *New York Times,* June 1, 1958.

White, Gordon. "Mantle Fractures Left Foot." *New York Times,* June 6, 1963.

Vecsey, George. "Sports of the Times." *New York Times,* January 30, 1994.

FILM

Great American Pastimes Company, *Baseball in the News: Volume 1, 1951-1955.* 1984.

WEB SITES

Baseball Almanac
http://www.baseball-almanac.com/

Baseball Links
http://www.baseball-links.com/

HeavyHitter.com (more baseball links)
http://www.heavyhitter.com/

Historic Baseball
http://www.historicbaseball.com/

Mickey Mantle

http://www.themick.com/

The National Baseball Hall of Fame & Museum

http://www.baseballhalloffame.org/

The Official Site of Major League Baseball

http://mlb.mlb.com/index.jsp

Tribute to Mickey Mantle

http://www.theswearingens.com/mick/

FURTHER READING

Buckley Jr., James. *Classic Ballparks.* New York: Barnes & Noble Books, 2004.

Christopher, Matt. *Great Moments in Baseball History.* New York: Little, Brown, 1996.

Gutman, Bill. *It's Outta Here! The History of the Home Run from Babe Ruth to Barry Bonds.* Dallas, Texas: Taylor Publishing Company, 2005.

MacKay, Claire. *Touching All the Bases: Baseball for Kids of All Ages.* Tonawanda, N.Y.: Firefly Books Ltd., 1996.

Morgan, Joe. *Baseball for Dummies.* Hoboken, N.J.: Wiley Publishing Inc., 2005.

Stout, Glenn. *Yankees Century: 100 Years of New York Yankees Baseball.* Boston: Houghton Mifflin, 2002.

WEB SITES

The Official Site of the New York Yankees
http://newyork.yankees.mlb.com

The Only Official Mickey Mantle Web site
http://www.theswearingens.com/mantle/

PICTURE CREDITS

INDEX

ABOUT THE AUTHOR

RONALD A. REIS is the author of 15 books, including young adult biographies of Eugenie Clark, Jonas Salk, and Lou Gehrig.